I AM NOT YOUR PREY

EMBRACING THE SKILLS, COURAGE, AND STRENGTH TO TAKE FLIGHT WITH BROKEN WINGS.

BOOK 1 of the Shattering Shame Series

ANDREA S. JONES

Library of Congress Control Number: 2022923302

ISBN: 979-8-88583-174-1 (Paperack)
ISBN: 979-8-88583-175-8 (Hardback)
ISBN: 979-8-88583-176-5 (Ebook)

From: Forgiveness: Unleashing the Extraordinary
by Yvonne Sotelo-Garcia

Shame becomes her—all of her. This label is horrifying and often offensive to others, but when one goes through a season of sexual abuse, it becomes their entire identity. Andrea Jones reveals her childhood experience. Caught in the web of her predator, known to others as a neighborly and kind man, she was reluctant to inform her family of this heinous crime because of the fear that no one would believe her. She channels this fear and energy to teach us how the grooming process works through her experience.

Many of you have reached a point of awareness and are looking for answers. For you, the reader, as you partake in her experience, remember you are not alone. Through Andrea's journey, you will understand her heart and why she is brave today to reveal her untold truth. Her heart yearns to reach victims of sexual abuse and teach the world what red flags to watch out for, so we as a community can protect the helpless. She is no longer a victim, but a victor! Her healing and broken heart were mended by the only answer that worked for her and many others - Jesus Christ, the son of God. "He heals the brokenhearted and binds up their wounds." (Psalm 147:3). I encourage you to soak in every page with an open heart and allow our Father in Heaven, Abba, to heal you from the inside out.

God bless you, Yvonne Sotelo-Garcia
Author Child of God
Sexual Abuse Survivor
MAED, BSP

NOTE TO THE READER

Dear Beautiful Reader,

The whole reason for sharing this story is you. You are precious, loved, and valued. Join me for a flight down memory lane as we go back in time and experience how a family becomes ensnared with a Predator. You won't find him particularly intimidating or forceful. He enters your life through the commonplace tasks of daily living. His character is chivalrous, helpful, and funny at times. You may find him welcoming and well-liked in his neighborhood. You will be surprised to see how he becomes a beloved part of the family.

Sexual abuse and domestic violence leave invisible marks. Long after the experience is over, you can have trouble finding purpose after you pick up

The spirit of the Sovereign Lord is on me, because the Lord has anointed me to proclaim good news to the poor. He has sent me to bind up the brokenhearted, to proclaim freedom for the captives and release from darkness for the prisoners, to proclaim the year of the Lord's favor and the day of vengeance of our God, to comfort all who mourn and to provide for those who grieve in Zion-to bestow on them a crown of beauty instead of ashes, the oil of joy instead of mourning, and a garment of praise instead of a spirit of despair. They will be called oaks of righteousness, a planting of the Lord for the display of his splendor.

Isaiah 61:1-3
(New International Version)

the pieces. It's messy. It can feel like your internal compass is broken. The all-consuming thread of connection I have found in every person I meet who has been a victim of this type of abuse is SHAME. Shame is a dream killer and a liar. It is paralyzing and keeps you feeling worthless. Shame stops you from pursuing your dreams and taking risks in your personal and professional life. Years go by, and you wonder why those around you thrive and seem to conquer one goal after another. You continue in that mediocre purposeless job or relationship that is safe but unfulfilling, or worse yet, dangerously dysfunctional. This is not God's plan for your life.

If you can relate to this on any level, this book series is for you. As you journey through this true story of some of life's tougher battlegrounds, you might just find answers to some of those "why" questions you have asked yourself for decades.

Along with the story here are some additional resources provided throughout the book.

REFLECTIONS

Utilizing outside resources and expanding on the text, you will see characteristics that make this family targets and coping mechanisms they develop to manage their life challenges.

STUDY GUIDE

You will find a study guide for each chapter at the back of the book. This will assist you in processing thoughts and feelings related to the content.

So, let's embrace the skills, courage, and strength to take flight with broken wings.

CONTENTS

FOREWORD

With a warm smile on her face and a tender and compassionate heart, you would never know the brokenness that once existed within her. Andrea is a beautiful, shining example of the healing that is possible after trauma and abuse. Not everyone finds their way to recovery.

Acknowledging trauma is difficult, and revisiting the past can be painful. Conscious awareness of those negative experiences inflicted upon us is necessary to break the chains that bind us and hold us back from living the life we deserve. Sadly, many avoid (or are afraid of) this "work" and live a life consumed by bad habits, unhealthy relationships, and self-inflicted shame. Andrea bravely shares her personal experience, pain, and learning in an honest and vulnerable way in an effort to bring about awareness and, at the same time, give hope to others.

Because there are so many who have had similar experiences, and one would never know from the smiles they wear, this is precisely why this book is so important, and the message is needed.

Now is the time to shatter shame and confidently embrace a future of personal fulfillment and positive possibilities! I encourage you to join Andrea on this beautiful journey of self-discovery and reflection, leading to a healthier, happier life.

—Shane Svorec

Mental health advocate, crisis intervention worker, and award-winning author of *Broken Little Believer* and *The Busy Bridge That Got Its Break*

STEPS OF GROOMING[1]

Target the victim

Gain the victim's trust

Gain the trust of the victim's family

Gain access and isolate the victim

Sexualize the relationship

Control and conceal the abuse

[1] Ron Meneo, "Sexual Abuse Lawsuits," AbuseLawsuit.com, October 28, 2021, https://www.abuselawsuit.com/.

1
OUTWITTED

I could smell him. My gut told me he was leering at me through the slightly cracked door. The scent of sweat and perversion permeated my nostrils. An animalistic sort of fragrance oozed out of him—not body odor, but an uncommonly distinct scent lingered. I thought to myself, "Perhaps it's pheromones? I remember my teacher talking about pheromones. Do they have an odor? I can't remember." I liken it to the way a particular smell connects to a memory, and it transports you through time in an instant. In my future, unfortunate men who carried a similar scent would be judged mercilessly in the courtroom of my mind.

The light *clickety-click* of my mother's heels marching down the hall brought an overwhelming blanket of dread to my soul. "Where was she going?" I asked myself. "Oh, why couldn't Tia stay over today?" I didn't move an inch.

As my mom called out, "Goodbye," I continued to feign sleep.

"How long would she be gone?" my desperate mind questioned me. "Could I keep up this charade for the duration of her absence?" It was unlikely.

The aggravation stirred inside my solar plexus, a slow-burning flame of nerves bubbling just under the surface. I knew it was waiting for unfortunate circumstances to fan it, to ignite it, encouraging its attempt to swallow me up.

Harry's voice echoed back to her as he called out, "Goodbye, see you later."

I flopped my head on the opposite side of the bed so he couldn't see my face through the door. Seeing me blink would alert him to the state of my consciousness.

My racing mind rebuked me, "Ok, think, Andrea, think. If I could just get to the phone somehow without him noticing. God, please strike him with a plague of diarrhea, or send somebody to knock on the door. Oh, please, please. What am I going to do?" If I could get Monique to come over, that would be golden. She had to finish her chores before leaving the house, but once she left home, she could be gone all day long without any backlash from her parents. My thoughts continued, "Maybe I could . . ."

CREAK.

Squeaky hinges on my bedroom door skidded my thoughts to a standstill.

"Andrea, are you awake?" Harry spoke in a croaked whisper.

"Oh my God, he is going to try to wake me up. I cannot believe it. He never wakes me up. Why did he want to wake me? I bet that means that Mom is not going to be gone all day."

"Andrea," he spoke again in that hushed, throaty voice. "Hey, you awake?"

I remained unmoving and still as death. Not moving, my brain seemed frozen. He thought I was awake. As my thoughts flowed slowly, I coached myself, "Stir, just a little, like people do when they hear noise in their sleep." Obeying, I moved slightly so my sleep would seem genuine. Still, I detected his unrelenting presence in my room. As if I could hear the rotors spinning in his mind, I perceived him watching me, assessing me. I languished, "God, how long was he going to stand there staring at me?"

Finally, in despair, I cried out with my whole heart, willing that someone would come. Somebody, anybody—Andy, my babysitter, or his brother Steve, the paperboy, or even annoying Bobby Horton from across the street. Hell, I even hoped for the Avon lady to knock on our door, but nobody came.

Suddenly, the swoosh of Harry's flip-flops sped across the square linoleum tiles and departed from my room. When we moved into this house, Mom and Harry gave my sister and me a choice of this bedroom or the carpeted bedroom. We chose this bedroom so I could conduct my obsession with the game of Jack's without having to sit on the kitchen floor. Secondly, with wheels on our bedframes, it was easier to push our beds out of the way so we could dance. The movie *Saturday Night Fever* had pushed disco dancing into the forefront of my free time with my friends, and I loved staging dance-offs in my room.

"Where did he go?" My thought subsided as I realized that the house was eerily silent. Listening intently for any indicator of where he was, I strained my ears while slightly tilting my head. "Maybe he went into the dayroom to watch TV?" I hoped in vain but knew better. The door to the dayroom frequently swelled and made a loud *clunk* when opening. I did not recall hearing that distinctive sound. No cupboard doors or refrigerator opening. Nothing. The bathroom was across the hall from my bedroom, and there was no sound there either. I lay still, eyes closed, for what seemed like forever. He must be out smoking.

I felt like a gerbil hiding from a snake in a glass box, knowing there was nowhere to hide but unable to stop pacing back and forth, back and forth while the snake watches lazily, slowly playing with you, knowing you can't win. I knew every inch of this house. I knew every squeak, every potential hiding place. I knew when I heard the slider in the dayroom that I could go from my room to the front door and quietly open and close it undetected before he made it into the living area. I knew that if I sat on the side of the house under the windowsill, I could see where Harry went and evade him if he went down the hallway. I also knew that If I pulled my knees up to my chest, I could squeeze my whole body inside the cupboard in the laundry room.

When forever turned into forever and five minutes, I decided it was safe to open my eyes. I didn't move my body because my head was facing the wall and the bedroom window, not the door. I instinctively knew it remained slightly cracked open even though Harry had attempted to make it sound like he closed it when he exited. My bedroom window had plants from the garden gently obstructing the view into the backyard patio and the pool but not completely. The light still shined beautifully above me and over onto the wall near the bedroom door next to my Bee Gees poster. I planned how to get to the phone in the living room while staring at the wall next to my bed. Against my will, my heartbeat escalated, and instantly I knew I had blown it.

Before my mind comprehended it, my body revealed he had outplayed me. As clever as I was, Harry had outwitted me. Though I perceived what I would see, I still couldn't stifle the scream as I edged my head upward. My eyes focused as Harry's two beady eyes came into view from behind the window screen, right between the date palm and spray of fern leaves. My vision was enhanced—the way a clip from a horror film pans in from a fuzzy global focus to a pinpoint of complete clarity—on his mocking smile as it connected with my terrified nine-year-old eyes.

REFLECTION

Coping Mechanisms

Active Listening: Andrea planned her days based on her family's activities so that she would not be alone with Harry. This required much of Andrea's time and thought life.

Strategic Thinking: Home became a battleground. Knowing every place to hide and what could be seen from every vantage point became a key strategy for avoiding sexual abuse.

The effect of developing these coping skills was that Andrea thought like someone much older than eight years old. She anticipated the future the way an adult might. This was viewed as maturity by authority figures in her life instead of the defense mechanism that it was.

2
HARRY

To understand how we got to this place, I must take you back to the beginning. I cannot pinpoint exactly when Harry came into our lives. Regrettably, I can tell you he became one of the most significant men in my life. When life's defining moments came at me, I ran to Harry. Harry had a magical way of explaining hard truths leaving you with a bittersweet feeling instead of the harsh crash reality can sometimes deliver. I confided in him when I realized that Santa Claus was not a chubby guy sliding down chimneys, and the Easter Bunny did not make it around the world delivering candy-laden baskets all in one night. Somehow, I came out of that conversation knowing that it was now my responsibility to carry on the spirit of giving and love that embodied those holidays. It felt like a rite of passage, and I felt honored to carry it.

Though I do not remember Harry moving into our home, I remember the day I met him. When I was seven years old, Harry came to dinner. "Answer the door, Andrea," Mom called out from the kitchen.

I took my time plodding down the hallway on my way to the door. I turned the handle and gently pulled the door toward myself while backing up before stepping into the doorway to view our guest. I hated him on sight. He had a very salesman-like demeanor and smiled too much, but his charisma was captivating. If I am honest, I will admit the thing I hated the most about him was that he was not my dad. Regardless of the reasons, my seven-year-old BS meter was going off like an ambulance siren.

I stood there staring at him without speaking until Mom's voice knocked me out of my reverie. "Don't just stand there; invite him in."

I turned around and saw Mom's glare before turning to Harry and mumbling come in.

"Charlene, go grab the salt and pepper and set it on the table," Mom said as she passed the placemats over the kitchen counter to me.

As we sat down to our meal, I recall staring into Harry's bubbly face with an expression of slightly veiled disgust. However, one look at my mom's stare wordlessly beating me down from behind the kitchen counter assured me that I had better wipe that expression from my face and replace it with something welcoming—Mom did not put up with ill manners or sassy children. I attempted a grimace and managed indifference.

A steady flow of light conversation flowed as we ate our meal. Harry told us a little bit about his family. He was the youngest of four children and he had grown up in La Mesa. His parents had purchased their home when the community of San Carlos was being built. They purchased the third house built on their street and had long standing ties in the community. Mom shared that we were also Native San Diegans and had been here for our whole lives and most of our extended family lived here as well.

"Andrea, you and your sister, clear the table, and then we will play a game." Mom said with a cheerful smile largely in my direction, attempting to coax me into doing the same. I obeyed.

The new guy had already charmed my little sister. He showed her a magic trick with a deck of cards he must have had in his pocket, and she was appropriately amused. I made observations as I joined my sister at the table. Harry smelled of nerves and sweat, showered in cologne, and his physique resembled the Pillsbury doughboy. Showing residuals of previous teenage acne, his face was a bit pockmarked. Even so, he had a warmth about him. His presence created a level of comfort that captured my sister, Charlene right away. She giggled and laughed, as he entertained her, she was clearly enamored with him.

I held my ground, determined not to succumb to his charms. He was on my turf and would be treated like a stray, uninvited dog If I had anything to say about it. Unfortunately, I did not. With the table cleared, we set up the board game, and the family became the new guy's captive audience. As much as I wanted to avoid interacting with him, I knew excusing myself from the game was not an option, so with a heavy sigh, I joined my sister for the after-dinner activity.

"It's your turn." I glanced over to see Charlene beaming sweetly as she handed me the little pegs to put into the car.

As I struggled to get the peg into the hole, she held out her hand, stating, "I will do it for you if you want."

"Ok," I answered flatly.

My mom beamed at every little joke Harry told, and Charlene mimicked that behavior. We girls were happy to have our mom in a good mood regardless of the reason. That was the one good thing about this little powwow in my mind. I hadn't been on my mom's best side lately and felt like I was walking on eggshells. Naturally, my sour mood had nothing to do with that.

Watching the little cars move around the game board, I continued with my stoic behavior. I was all in now, fully vested. There was no turning back, and no smiles would crack out of this face. There was just one problem: Harry was completely unaffected. He didn't care one iota that I was shunning him. Nor did he try harder or direct his attention my way, hoping for me to throw him a bone. He simply ignored me. It was unbelievable. He seemed amused by my antics.

When my mom asked if we wanted ice cream bars and I declined, he ate mine too. "I'll take it," he stated, smiling widely with his huge, toothy smile.

It was infuriating. The game took an eternity to end. When Mom excused us and encouraged us to head off to bed, I was delighted and sped off like a Nascar finalist on the last lap. No long goodnights here. My sister tried to get a few more minutes out of her, and I heard her run to get her artwork to show Harry what she had done that week in school.

Throwing myself onto my bed, the tears of frustration rolled down my face. I hastily yanked on my nightgown and hopped into my bed, feeling completely defeated. The angry energy that had driven me all night fizzled out of me like a slow leak in a bicycle tire. With the dissipation of those strong, aggressive feelings, I only had this unrelenting sadness that permeated my heart like a nebulous black cloud, ready to strike me down. I knew it would surround me and swallow me up until there was nothing left of me but the shards of my heart. It felt like little pieces of broken glass on the ground that get swept up and thrown into the garbage can when something is unfixable.

REFLECTION

Grooming Step One: -Target the Victim

Vulnerabilities

Andrea was angry and depressed about her parent's divorce, and she felt little control in her life. The attitude she displayed toward Harry was more related to her missing her father and her fear of her life changing even further. There were needs that were not being met, and the family was in a vulnerable position, making them an easy target for Harry. They were looking for security and stability. Charlene welcomed Harry's fun, relaxed demeanor and viewed him positively.

Even Andrea observed her Mom's lift in mood during the date. However, she was looking back towards her father as the provider of security and stability, and she saw Harry as a threat to her hopes of her parents reuniting.

3

MOM

It was Saturday, and Mom had slept in. I wanted to go outside and ride my bike, so I pulled on my favorite pair of jeans that were so worn out I was only allowed to wear them to play in.

Pushing my feet into my sneakers with no socks, I inched her bedroom door open very slowly to see if she was awake.

"Mom," I whispered in a hushed voice. "Can I go ride my bike?"

"If you take your sister with you." Mom mumbled.

"She doesn't want to ride bikes. Can't she just play in the room?" Disappointed, I threw the words out there, knowing it was not a promising idea.

"Do you want to go or not?" Mom snapped.

"Ok, I will take her with me," I said as I began retreating out of the room.

"Wait a minute." Mom sat up and looked at me. "Go get me a pen and a piece of paper."

I retrieved the items she asked for, and she jotted a quick note: "Please allow Andrea to purchase one pack of Marlboro Lights." She signed the bottom of the sheet before handing it back to me.

"Walk down to 7-Eleven and get me some cigarettes, and then you can ride your bike." Pushing money into my hand, she lay back on the pillows and turned onto her side.

7-Eleven was down the street from our apartment. Most of the cashiers knew me, and they took my note and gave me the cigarettes without any trouble, as my mom regularly sent me in to retrieve her cigarettes while she waited in the car. I took the little bag and headed out of the store.

Walking home from the store, I thought about our dinner with Harry. The details of the conversation replayed in my mind. I could hear Harry asking, "What do you like in school? Let me see your artwork. Do you want to see a card trick?"

As I relived his jokes and reassessed his easy-going personality, an intense longing for my dad overtook me. I couldn't help but think that if Dad were here, I wouldn't have to take Charlene with me everywhere I went. It seemed that since Dad left, I couldn't do anything without her, and a wave of resentment towards my Mom washed over me.

After delivering the package, my mom let me go out and ride my bike without my sister. When I was doing my errand, a neighbor kid had asked if Charlene could play with her, so I was off the hook. Elated, I walked towards the other side of the complex with my bicycle, which was entirely too big for me.

The building that we lived in was part of a subsidized housing program through HUD. This particular building housed Native American people needing assistance. Charlene and I were struggling to fit in with the Native American children our age that also lived in the housing.

There was a core group from the housing of roughly seven kids that walked the same route to school as we did. Shortly after we moved into the apartment, they made it clear that they felt we didn't belong there. Our Mom was 90% Native American but our father was all Caucasian. Our lighter skin put a target on our backs.

The phrases, "Go home white girl" and "You don't belong here" were frequently shouted at us. I tried to steer clear of them while walking to school and playing outside. I ignored their taunts but last week during the walk to school the aggression escalated from verbal jabs to physical attack. I was walking alone without Charlene that day and they began throwing rocks at me. I ran but they chased me, and I had huge bruises on my arm where the rocks hit me. Before going to class, I went to the bathroom crying. A classmate saw my arm and my tears and told our teacher Mrs. Everett. She pulled me up in front of the class and pointing at my arm she rebuked the class for the bullying. I had felt embarrassed and humiliated.

With the harassment I had been experiencing I tried not to play near our building. There was a short brick wall near the sidewalk on the north side of the complex, and I used it to stand on while I mounted onto my bicycle seat and pushed off pedaling. After some time riding up and down the walkway, I circled to the opposite side of the complex and found the apartment of Kerri, a girl I knew from school. Kerri and I had been playing together for the last few weeks. I liked her and was happy to have finally found a friend

Much to my dismay, this past Friday, a few mean girls at school had made fun of my homemade clothes, and instead of sticking up for me, Kerri pretended she didn't know me. My grandmother loved to sew and made some things for Charlene and me. I was proud of my new outfits, and had invited Kerri in and shown them to her. Showing off my new clothes I told her that I avoided wearing the items Grandma had made me previously because the material was itchy, but I really liked these.

As I showed her my new collection she said, "Oh, I love this one." The dress material was satiny and had a large paisley print. She went on picking up another dress, "This looks like a dress Jan from the Brady Bunch would wear." At seven years old we were beginning to become aware of fashion and trendy clothes brands.

We had enjoyed picking through my new stuff and I went to school on Friday with a little skip in my step wearing a pair of corduroy bell bottoms and a loose blouse from grandma's gifts. My joy diminished when the girl's made fun of me. What really hurt was the realization that they wouldn't have known my clothes were homemade if Kerri hadn't told them.

Kerri had hurt my already raw feelings. Every avenue I explored trying to make friends seemed to lead to loneliness and rejection. I felt so betrayed and helpless to change my circumstances. Suddenly, I had a burning desire to hurt her right back. The front door to her apartment was open, allowing the breeze to blow in despite the cool weather, but her screen door was closed. I knocked, but nobody answered. Hearing movement inside, I felt sure Kerri was there but ignoring me. With a deep sigh, I backed away from the door.

The sidewalk formed a large circle in front of her door as this was where each building of the complex met, so the sidewalk circled and veered off in four different directions. I began riding around the paved circular sidewalk chanting, "Kerri is a bitch; Kerri is a bitch," thinking she would hear me and come outside so I could confront her.

Even as I did it, I wondered why I was doing it. I didn't even understand myself.

After making two passes around, chanting my phrase, Karma made a hasty appearance. I hit an unfortunately placed rock and toppled over, falling off my bike onto the manicured grass in the middle of the circle. I heard a screen door open, and a woman, who I soon learned was Kerri's mom, helped me up.

She stared pointedly down at me and commanded, "Go home and do not come back, or I will go talk to your mother. Where did you learn to talk like that, anyhow?"

Having no clever response and terrified at the idea of her speaking to my mom, I held back tears and gave a weak apology, then turned around, walking my bike towards my apartment since I couldn't get onto the seat without the aid of the brick wall.

As I pushed towards home, I felt so defeated. A slight sense of shame washed over me because of my unkind behavior, but underneath it all, I felt a gnawing loneliness. Kerri was my only friend who lived in my complex; now I had none. The hurt masked as anger exuded from me in the form of a salty expression and aggressive gestures. To top it all off, it started to sprinkle. I threw my bike down on the ground a bit too forcefully and stomped into the apartment, feeling more frustrated than ever.

I didn't have time to wallow as I was snapped back into the present by my mom's voice. "Go outside and find your sister. It's about to rain, and I don't want her catching a cold."

"Ok." I answered back as I picked up my windbreaker.

Grabbing a spoon from the kitchen, I headed back outside. I loved digging for worms when it was rainy. The dirt was moist, and it was easy to get a few layers under the ground where the good earthworms resided without bending my spoon. Running up the apartment sidewalk, I turned the opposite way of my sister's friend Ruth's apartment. I went to the other side of the complex, where the water pooled, and the earth would already be getting soft.

I spent about ten minutes digging for worms before the sprinkles turned into larger raindrops. Abandoning my dig, I continued towards Ruth's house. Running toward my destination, I slipped, soaking my pant leg with mud. Jumping up, I dusted myself off. Finally, I knocked on Ruth's door, and her brother answered.

Before I could ask, he spouted out, "Charlene went home when it started sprinkling." Then he shut the door.

Hurrying down the path, I scuttled my way back to our door. Before I could get my wet windbreaker off, I felt my body being ushered down the hall and pushed into the bathroom by a quick yank of my arm.

"What did I tell you?" my mom bellowed at me.

I stared in abject stillness, paralyzed into silence by the angry look on her face.

"I said to go get your sister and bring her home out of the rain. Where did you go?"

"I went to get my sister," I quietly replied.

"Don't lie to me," my mom yelled, even though we were inches apart. "Get in your room right now." Her voice pierced the air as she pushed me from the bathroom down the hall toward the room I shared with my sister. "And take those dirty pants off," she added as I got through the bedroom door.

I didn't get my windbreaker off before my mom came barreling into my room, "I thought I told you to clean up this mess."

"I did." My voice cracked as I looked desperately around. There wasn't anything out of place that I could see.

"Get up," she yelled.

I jumped off the bed, and she bent down and yanked all the objects from under the bed. Toys that had no place or didn't fit in the toybox got pulled viciously from underneath the bed.

"Where does this go?" She began pushing the items in question into my arms faster than I could catch them, and they dropped to the floor. "Not under the bed," she snarled.

"I don't know where to put it," I responded, feeling distressed.

I felt the sting of a slap across my face before I saw her hand move. She walked over to my dresser, where items were placed on top, and with one fell swoop of her arm, wiped everything onto the floor. "Get this mess cleaned up, and don't let me catch you putting it under the bed, or I am going to give you a beating you won't forget. Maybe that will help you remember to do things right." With that, she turned and walked out of the room, leaving me with the aftermath of her outburst to clean.

Dejected, I circled around, taking in the state of the room. Overwhelm smothered me. Tears streamed down my face as I bent down to pick up an item off the floor.

REFLECTION

Effects of Divorce

An article titled "The Effects of Parental Divorce on Children,"[2] by Huseyin Çaksen states that children whose families are going through a divorce have higher percentages of developing emotional and behavioral disorders, including depression and even suicide.

Hurting children will find an outlet for their pain. -Andrea displayed her hurt by lashing out at her only friend and further alienating herself. After their parents' divorce, they relocated, and Charlene and Andrea had to make new friends. Her behavior only intensified the loneliness she was feeling.

Abusive behavior is passed from generation to generation.

In an article titled "Mental Health: Dissociative Amnesia" from WebMD[3], it is stated that dissociative amnesia can be

---

[2]   Huseyin Çaksen, "The Effects of Parental Divorce on Children," Psychiatrike = Psychiatriki (U.S. National Library of Medicine, November 26, 2021), https://pubmed.ncbi.nlm.nih.gov/34860682/.

[3]   WedMD Editorial Contributors, "Mental Health: Dissociative Amnesia," WebMD (WebMD, April 21, 2021), https://www.webmd.com/mental-health/dissociative-amnesia.

triggered by trauma and causes people to block out specific information. Oddly enough, Andrea's mother did not recall behaving like this toward Andrea or Charlene, though it happened many times. She did, however, share stories of her own mother ripping through the room and wiping everything off the dressers and nightstands.

4

MEET THE FAMILY

"Hi," I yelled as I happily flung myself into my grandfather's arms.

I called my grandfather Bepop and my grandmother Memo. We had not visited their house in two or three weeks, and I was thrilled to spend the day with them.

In my excitement, I shouted, "Hurry up!" at my sister trailing behind me.

Charlene dawdled, entering about thirty seconds after me with Mom and Harry meandering behind.

There was an indescribable comfort I experienced at my grandparents' home I didn't experience anywhere else. Unconditional welcome was a permanent fixture here, and it was my redemption more than once. The door always remained unlocked—I cannot recall a time when my grandparents didn't have at least one relative staying with them. Sometimes it was a cousin attending college or one of my uncles. At times, it was us. No matter how you sliced it up, there were always a sizable number of bodies there. In all honesty, I believe my grandfather could have done without all of us there all the time, but my grandmother kept us close. She would never close the door on a family member, and we

19

all knew it, so when tough times hit, we showed up at the door, and they created space for us.

My grandparents had not met Harry yet. Bepop welcomed everybody. He thought the best of you until you gave him a reason not to, and even then, he didn't show his displeasure. Memo was a different story. My mom was barely in the door when Memo set the tone.

She greeted Mom with, "Well, just look at that girl," referring to my sister. "What have you been feeding her? My God, she is so thin."

Charlene was anemic, so she looked a little pale, and it was true that she was very thin. That wasn't new, but my grandmother never missed an opportunity to point it out.

This was the pattern. Out of the corner of my eye, I spied my mom's face crinkling up with hurt that quickly turned to anger, and I thought, "Oh no, here we go." Mom would retaliate, and the tension would set in and permeate the room like a damp towel. The fun afternoon I had pictured in my mind turned into a scene from a bad B-rated movie you can't stop yourself from watching even though it doesn't get any better.

My mom promptly opened her mouth to defend herself against the verbal jabs, but before she could speak, Harry looked at my grandmother, smiled a bit too sweetly, and replied, "Well, we let her out of the closet to visit today, and we fed her yesterday. She even got water with her lump of coal."

A stunned silence hung in the air. Five seconds passed, and then Bepop started laughing, bellowing from deep down inside himself. It was contagious. One after another, unable to keep it inside, we all burst into raucous laughter. Even Mom joined in. Memo looked gob-smacked and, making a sour face, stomped off toward the kitchen.

This felt like a wonderful, new first in our visits with the Grands. I do not remember my grandmother commenting on my sister's height, weight, or general paleness any time after that visit. Harry set precedence, and it changed the whole dynamic of our family interactions.

"Perhaps, he wasn't so bad after all?" I thought.

"How is everybody doing?" my uncle Bill asked as he patted my head on his way into the kitchen. Uncle Bill and Aunt Francis arrived shortly after we did. They retained an easy kinship with my grandparents. A love of going to movies and traveling to Vegas seemed to unite them.

My grandmother had crafted an art of making you think and feel the other people in the family were her favorites. During that season, we all thought Aunt Francis was her favorite, though I am positive that Aunt Francis did not share our perception. Charlene was the only person that honestly believed she was my grandmother's favorite, and she was correct. They had a special bond. Memo loved us all fiercely, but she displayed it differently than the stereotypical cookie-baking grandmother. It wasn't until I was fully grown that I grasped the depth of her devotion to all of us.

My grandfather, on the other hand, made everybody think they were his favorite. I knew I truly was his favorite, and I was correct. I was Bepop's girl, and nothing I requested from him was denied. Everything from pancakes for breakfast, trips to the community pool I adored, and he detested, and outings to the taco shop. As an adult, he bought me my first car. My father supported us financially via child support; however, he was absent from our lives. Bepop's example displayed how a good man should live, how a man provides for his family, and how children and women should be treated.

Bepop entertained us with a magic trick and pulled a few quarters out of our ears before Uncle Bob made an appearance. "Andrea, come on over here and take a look at this." He was holding out an Indian nickel he had pulled out of his pocket.

Uncle Bob was great with little kids. He always had a significant item of interest to show my sister and me. One time, it was an ancient rock from a volcano that had allegedly erupted and destroyed a whole civilization. Another, it was an uncommon sampling of fruit I had never experienced, like dragon fruit or papaya. He once carted my sister and me, along with our cousins, to the tidepools where we explored the mossy rocks, searching out hidden starfish and other sea creatures.

There was an extremely specific window of special favor from Uncle Bob. Once we developed opinions of our own—at roughly pre-teen age—he wouldn't entertain us again until we grew up. Aunt Suzanne, Uncle Bob's wife, was much better with us as we got to be pre-teens. She would entertain us with nail parties and popcorn when we got to hang out with her and our cousins before she and Uncle Bob divorced.

The last to arrive was Uncle Jimmy. "Hey, get out of the way! You're blocking the path to the food," he said and gently shoved me aside as he beelined to the stove to sneak a bite from the covered dishes of food waiting to be placed on the table.

He is ten years older than me and ten years younger than my mom. Jimmy spent extensive time babysitting my sister and me. Riding on the handlebars of his bicycle and cruising the neighborhood is a favorite of my childhood memories. Thinking back, I still smell the freshly cut grass next to the apartment stairs and I can feel the hard handlebars on my hips as the bicycle bumped down each stair with me bobbing up and down straining to hold on. Uncle Jimmy had me convinced that there was a monster in the closet that took up a permanent residence there.

Tickle torture and hanging spit over my face were also commonplace. Later, after he obtained his driver's license, we spent many afternoons in the waves on the front of his surfboard.

There was a stable level of camaraderie as we sat at the table to enjoy an early dinner. A big pot of beans had been cooking all afternoon, and there were fresh tortillas, seasoned meat, fried potatoes, homemade salsa, and a cucumber salad. Being with my extended family felt so good; I temporarily forgot the sadness that had permeated my being as of late, and I genuinely enjoyed the day. Even Harry's presence did little to dampen the mood.

After dinner, I went out to the backyard and picked plums off the tree. They were so juicy and delicious. I fell promptly asleep during the car ride home, thinking of how much I relished days like this.

REFLECTION

In this chapter, you see steps two and three of the grooming process: Gain the Victim's Trust and the Trust of the Victim's Family.

Grooming Step Two: Gain the Victim's Trust

Having a place where you feel loved unconditionally can be the difference between being an overcomer or being overcome. For Andrea, this place was her grandparent's home. Each person there had an impact on her life, and she felt safe. Harry entered that safe haven and immediately began building a connection there.

Grooming Step Three: Gain the Trust of the Victim's Family

Harry very effectively diffused the tension between Andrea's Mother, Theda and Memo. By adding this value, he made the visit more comfortable for everyone. He succeeded in making a good first impression and opened the door of acceptance into the family.

5

AND THEN THERE WERE FOUR

People in the neighborhood called our apartment complex the "blue roofs." The building had a new coat of paint, which covered up the flaws in the construction. Smatterings of bushes popped up throughout the complex that ran parallel to the sidewalk. Our apartment was on the second floor of the tall, slightly weathered three-story building. As our door faced a large parking lot, the view left something to be desired.

I don't recall precisely when Harry moved in with us. There was no striking moment of his coming into our home with his stuff, unpacking boxes, or even the lifestyle adjustments that come from bringing in an additional person. I just remember he was there.

I equate his arrival with Halloween. There is a picture of me in my costume that year, standing in front of my painted bedroom door. That door is such a wonderful tidbit of happiness in my mind. Our excitement was boundless when my mom removed the door from its hinges and announced that we were going to embark on a home project. My sister and I spent a whole Saturday with our mom sketching outlines of flowers on the door and then painting them.

Creativity is guaranteed to bring out the best in my mom. She was happiest when she was creating something—and I clearly remember how joyful she was that day.

Mom usually made our Halloween costumes. A wonderful feeling comes with knowing that what you imagine or describe would be achieved exactly as you imagined it. Mom captured my vision perfectly every time. This particular year I was a princess. The dress was beautiful satiny smooth, baby blue material overlaid with flowing chiffon that came in at the waist and poofed out and down like the Cinderella gown in the old Disney animated version of the movie. I had a crown that sparkled like no other. I now know it was made of cardboard and tin foil with some glitter glued onto it, but to my seven-year-old self, it was the most beautiful dress on the planet. I felt like royalty wearing it.

I heard a scream and went outside just in time to see the backside of a little kid dropping his candy as he ran. Harry had also gleaned the benefit of my mom's costume creations. He stood outside next to the menacing cauldron emitting a bubbling fog from the dry ice inside. Dressed as Igor, he had green skin from head to toe and a hunchback. He wore a torn long-sleeved Pendleton shirt that appeared bloody and shredded jeans cut off right above his ankles, showing his bare feet. A stuffed pillowcase strapped to his torso underneath the Pendleton created the misshapen back. He had blackened several of his teeth, and his hair was disheveled—he looked terrifying. Small children and even some older kids had panic-stricken expressions when the realization dawned on them that they couldn't get by our apartment door without passing within a foot of him. Mom dressed as a witch with green skin and wore a long black gown. She had a wart on the tip of her nose, and a tall, pointed hat and black teeth made her almost as attractive as Harry.

"Hey, are you ready?" Harry displayed his black teeth at me. "Get your sister. Your mom is going to walk with you. I will stay here and pass out the candy. When you girls get back, we will head over to your grandparents' house."

I was having so much fun watching Mom and Harry scaring the kids I forgot we planned to go to Memo and Bepop's. We went there every year and trick or treated around their neighborhood.

There was a decent amount of candy collected after hitting all three floors of our building and most of the bottom floors of the other buildings. Mom was not up for going up all the stairs. She watched Charlene and I hit the second floor of one of the other buildings, but after that, we stuck to the ground floor.

When we got back to our apartment, Mom collected sweaters for us. The temperature had dropped, and we still had a whole neighborhood to get candy from.

"Here go pour the rest of the candy into the big plastic bowl," Mom said handing us the remainder of the candy for distribution.

"We should put it in our bags," I said to Charlene as I poured the candy into the bowl.

After putting a few pieces in each of our bags, we placed the large bowl outside our door with a note saying, "Take two pieces." Not likely, but we hoped people would share.

Charlene and I couldn't wait to show Memo and Bepop our costumes. Bouncing in the door, I pushed ahead of Charlene to show off my costume.

"Wow, look at that crown," Bepop generously gushed over me.

Charlene was a hobo that year and had a little sack at the end of a stick she was carrying.

"Here, let me keep that for you while you walk the neighborhood." Memo held out her hand to retrieve Charlene's stick.

Memo had us stand in the front yard for some pictures before shooing us on our way. We had to get around the neighborhood and get home in time to take baths and get to bed as close to our bedtime as possible. Halloween was not going to change our bedtime, so we hurried to get from house to house.

"Come on Charlene," Let's go. I was eager to get as much candy as we could before it was time to go home.

Charlene stayed close to me as we took off running up the sidewalk.

Mom was great with keeping us on a schedule, helping us with our homework, and sticking to a routine. However, the weight of it was heavy on her. She often felt tired; her joy zapped from life because of the divorce from my father and the responsibility of raising two girls alone. Our grandparents provided support through babysitting, school pick-ups, and occasionally financial help. They were amazing and loved having us with them, but the relationship with my grandmother was a constant strain on my mother.

With Harry living with us, Mom had more support and didn't require as much assistance from them. The emotional lift brought out my mother's creative, joyful side, and my sister and I were happy to share in those benefits of his presence in our home.

REFLECTION

In this chapter you see steps three and four of the grooming process: Gain Trust and Access to the Victim

Gaining Trust

Providing support and easing Theda's load endeared Harry to the family. He participated in the family activity of dressing up for Halloween and making things fun and lighthearted.

Gaining Access
    Harry now resided in the home of his targeted victims.

6
VACATION

"Finish packing up your bags before dinner time. I will be in before dinner to check and be sure that you haven't forgotten anything. Remember toothbrushes, bathing suits and both of you bring your books. It is going to be a lot of driving, and you are going to want something to occupy your time," Mom said as she busied herself with packing her own bags.

"Ok, Mom," I hollered back down the hallway.

"Be sure and help your sister too." Mom's voice faded as she headed into the bathroom to pack the toiletries we needed for our trip.

We were going on a summer vacation, and the excitement was bubbling because we had never been on a vacation before. Charlene and I had spent much of the afternoon out shopping with Mom. We picked out some new summer clothes for our trip and snacks to fill the cooler. Our choices were hard salami, French bread, yogurt, peanut butter crackers, Oreo cookies, and juice boxes. This trip was going to be fun!

Laying in our beds Charlene asked, "What do you think Las Vegas is like?"

"I know it has those slot machines like that little bank that we have, but I don't know what else is there." I answered thoughtfully.

Charlene said, "Do you think it's like Disneyland?"

"The place we are staying is called Circus Circus, so maybe they have circus animals." As I answered her, I imagined lions and tigers putting on a show for us.

"You girls go to sleep," Mom called from down the hallway. "We are leaving early in the morning, and I don't want to see any cranky faces."

I tossed back and forth in my bed, but soon enough, I dropped off to sleep, thinking of the adventure we headed towards. The sunlight peeked through my curtain as morning arrived, and I popped up ready to go. Our packed bags sat stacked near the front door. Before leaving, we ate an easy breakfast of buttered toast and jam with some crisp green apple slices served on paper plates for easy clean-up.

Bepop would be at the door any minute. We were using his truck with the camper shell, and we couldn't wait to lay claim to our places in the back. It would be fun riding back there without my mom and Harry. The independence of it all left me feeling grown up at the ripe age of eight Harry had only been with us for a few short months, but it felt longer.

It wasn't long before Bepop arrived. He showed Harry a few minor quirks the truck had. "See this light here on the dashboard? It stays on most of the time, so don't wait on that to check the fluids. Just check them regularly, and this old girl should run just fine. The lock on this door needs to be massaged just so to get it unlocked." Bepop spoke as he slid around the truck's perimeter, pointing and buffing at areas that needed attention.

After all these little foibles got worked out, we piled into the back of the camper and headed out for our first family vacation. It was really happening! As we headed down the highway toward Las Vegas, the adrenaline wore off and a level of contentment settled in. My sister and I played *Go Fish*—in the back of the camper as we bumped along.

"Do you have a four?" I asked.

"Go Fish," Charlene responded.

I enjoyed myself so much that I didn't even mind taking care of my sister.

Since Harry came crashing into our world, things had changed. We were becoming a family, as I had always desired. The resentment that my own father wasn't there had not completely dissipated, but the pain of it didn't feel so sharp and edgy. It was more of something that lingered in the background that I could call upon if necessary. I found myself unleashing that resentment less and less. Feelings were still very tentative about Harry, but there was no denying he was becoming somebody I didn't detest. Though I was not yet ready to fully embrace it, I genuinely enjoyed having him around.

After three hours of driving, we pulled over in a tiny town called Barstow. Harry opened up the door to the camper and let Charlene and I out. We stretched and used the restroom at a gas station and market.

"Can we get something to eat?" I asked Harry.

"Did you eat all of your snacks?" he asked.

"No, we want a sandwich though." I looked up at him and said, "Please can we have one?"

Charlene joined in. "Yes, a sandwich please."

"All right. Come on." Harry walked us into the market deli, and we got sandwiches before piling back into the camper and heading on our way.

Las Vegas was so exciting. We pulled into town as the sun sank into oblivion to take its rest as the evening began to lay claim to the city. A brilliant cascade of reds and burnt oranges lingered in the desert sky as she gracefully took her leave.

"Wow, look at all of the lights," I pointed out the camper window as we drove past hotel after hotel." Charlene and I stared in awe.

Finally, we pulled into the parking lot of Circus Circus. The hotel seemed like its own city towering up into the night sky, stealing its glory. Charlene and I waited in the camper as Harry and Mom checked in. We gathered our belongings and put our books and cards scattered about from the ride neatly back into our bags as we prepared to undertake the march up to our room.

We were intentionally close to the first floor because that floor and the second floor, was a playroom for kids. It felt like being at a carnival.

After checking in, Mom went up to the room and Harry came and got Charlene and me. We grabbed our suitcases and followed him into the Hotel. Charlene and I stared at the people coming and going. As we followed Harry towards the elevator, we heard the sounds of bells dinging and music coming from the casino floor. An announcers voice came over the intercom. He was introducing performers for a show that was just starting.

"Can we go look?" Charlene and I pulled on Harry's hands repeating "Please, can we just look really quick."

Harry smiled at us, turned away from the elevators and walked towards the casino floor where all of the commotion was happening saying "Come on girls, let's go check this out."

As we entered the casino floor the announcer stopped talking. We saw a small area with tiered benches quickly filling up with people eager to watch the show.

"What is that "Look up there," Charlene pointed towards the ceiling.

As we looked up the lights dimmed, and a spotlight shined on a man launching off of a small platform into the air holding a small bar attached to ropes hanging from the ceiling. We stared in wonder as he pulled himself up and hung his legs over the bar and continued swinging through the air hanging upside down. Next a girl launched off of a platform from the other side of the auditorium and let go of the bar she was swinging from and flew through the air before the man caught her hands and they hung in the air together. We set down our suitcases where we stood and watched in awe until they were done performing.

The show lasted fifteen minutes. When it was over Harry looked down at us saying, "Pick up your suitcases girls, your Mom will wonder where we are."

Finally in our room, we got cleaned up and hurried downstairs to the buffet for dinner. I could not believe the extravagant multitude of food choices that lay before us. Don't get me wrong; we ate well at home. My mom always cooked great meals but seeing all these choices was awe-inspiring.

Shrimp was my favorite, and the idea that I could just eat it to my heart's content was a novelty. They had pizza, pasta, prime rib, and ham with all the fixings, and they never ran low. A constant influx of fresh food replaced the barely eaten food that had gotten cold. It seemed wasteful to me even at eight years old, and right as I wondered what they did with the food not eaten, I reached the dessert table. Every delicious treat I could imagine spread out before me as I had never experienced.

"Look at the cheesecake," Harry said as he was picking up a piece of cheesecake and piling whip cream on top of it. There were brownies, pie, and huge pieces of chocolate cake. You couldn't make this stuff up. I was having the best time of my life, and this day was going down in the diary.

After our gluttonous dinner we went up to our hotel room.

"Hey, look in here." There was a desk drawer and it had small crayon boxes and coloring books. I pulled them out to show Charlene and then we ran around the room opening up every drawer to see what was inside. We found a pad and pen for taking notes and a Gideon bible. Next, we went into the bathroom to take baths before bed. There were little bottles of bubble bath and shampoo, and little wrapped up bars of soap.

The bathtub was big and had jets like a jacuzzi. Charlene and I both hopped in and played in the bubbles until Mom made us get out and put our pajamas on. When we went to crawl into bed there were little chocolate mints on top of our pillows. Just as we finished unwrapping them Mom said, "Don't eat those. You just brushed your teeth. You can save them for tomorrow." And she tucked us into our bed.

Charlene and I slept late. Partially because we were tired from the trip but also because the curtains kept the light out. I woke up first and then Charlene. Orange juice and donuts were on the table in the little kitchenette.

"Can we go play in the arcade?" I asked Mom

"After breakfast I will take you." Mom answered.

"I want to play that bowling game," Charlene looked at me as she spoke.

"ok. I want to play that pinball game and watch the trapeze artists again."

"Yeah, that was so cool," Charlene smiled as we talked.

We gulped down breakfast and got dressed so we could go play games. Mom and Harry bought us wristbands so we could play all day without putting quarters in the games. We even got popcorn and drinks without paying. When it was time for the next trapeze show, we sat on the benches in the viewing area eating popcorn.

After three days at Circus Circus, we were all tired of smoky air, machines clanging the too-familiar "*ding ding ding*," and being indoors. The thrill was gone, so we ate our last buffet breakfast and headed out for the next destination on our list.

Sequoia National Park's massive redwoods are some of the most beautiful trees on earth. We sat in awe as we drove right through the center of one of these majestic perennials through a hole in the middle of the trunk. The forest canopies created a protective hedge that enveloped us in an ecosystem of beauty and greenery. Even though it seemed that there was no open space in the foliage, the road curved, and there was an open field. We were in a place of wonder. The light edging through the treetops made this a perfect hide-n-seek location.

After setting up camp, we created a home base and headed out into the glorious forest to hide from Harry, who was elected to be "it." Mom and Harry were both experienced campers. They coached Charlene and me on using landmarks, finding water and shelter, and getting our sense of direction if we got lost. They assessed our skills by walking around our camp and challenging us to locate landmarks from each direction. Once we proved we could find our way back to camp, we began the game. I had no fear as a child and headed out to find a hiding place nobody would discover. Charlene did not share my sense of adventure and went with my mom, and they found hiding spots together.

In retrospect, the square footage of the area we hid in was not as large as my childhood perception led me to believe, but it felt like miles of the freedom I craved. After the game, we stoked a campfire and cooked our dinner on a grate over the open flame. Our hamburgers were so flavorful and juicy. We ate them with fruit and chips. As I slurped down the last drops in my juice box, the peacefulness settled in like an old friend and restored something inside of me I didn't know needed filling.

"Can we roast Marshmallows?" I asked Mom after we cleaned up the after-dinner plates and cups.

"Go get the hangers out of the camper."

"Yes!" Charlene and I ran to the camper and got out the wire hangers that we brought. Harry helped us bend them at the ends to make handles. Everybody got one.

We moved our folding chairs near the campfire and attached our marshmallows to our hangers. Harry got two lanterns out and put kerosene in them and lit the wicks. He placed one on the table behind Mom and handed her a book of poems by Edgar Allen Poe. Mom began reading the cremation of Sam McGhee.

We spent the next few days reading, playing games, and going on hikes. After one of us carelessly left some scraps behind, attracting the attention of some unwanted critters, Mom talked to us about putting away every bit of food in the cooler after each snack and meal. Harry wrapped a bungee cord around the cooler in the evening to ensure it stayed closed, and we managed to avoid future episodes with the local wildlife.

"Ouch, I can't stop scratching. It itches," I complained showing my Mom the red welts on my arms and legs. She went into the Rubbermaid tub with the medicine and toiletries and came back with calamine lotion. I was all pink, but I felt better.

"Do you have any Charlene?" Mom pulled her close and inspected her body for bites. Charlene had a few but not as many as I had.

The mosquitos continued to feast on us at every given opportunity. Off spray proved necessary, so we took a trip to the closest market on the campground and sprayed vigorously multiple times a day.

Something about being in nature brings communion with our creator to our hearts. I can still think back on this time in the Redwoods and recall the feeling of awe and connection this experience fostered. Knowing you are a part of something greater than yourself brings a sense of mystery to life, and that experience sparked in me a burning desire to find all life's secrets.

The third leg of our trip proved to be the most impactful. Bepop and Memo, along with Uncle Jimmy, met us in Yosemite. As an adult looking back, this was one of my most cherished trips with my family. It's funny how you don't realize the impact of the trivial things when they are happening, but when those people who were so essential in your young life are gone, the details suddenly loom large in your memory.

"Let's go, Andrea." Early the first day in Yosemite, Bepop walked me to the nearby stream. "Here, hold on to this." Handing me a medium-sized branch, he attached a small hook to a long piece of rough white string. He then applied a small piece of bacon onto the hook, and voila, we had a fishing pole.

I had never fished before, so I chattered incessantly when we didn't catch a fish in the first two minutes, bombarding Bepop with my questions. How long does it take? Why did we use bacon?

What happens when we catch a fish? I still remember Bepop looking at me with his lovingly amused expression as he responded in kind, modeling the patience the task required.

About ten minutes went by, and jumping up and down, I began screaming, "We caught one! Are we going to cook it?" I stared at it, wiggling on the line. It looked like an oversized goldfish, but to me, it was a masterpiece.

"We have to put it back. It's too small to cook." Bepop grinned as he removed the tiny fish from the hook.

I only felt slightly disappointed when we had to release the fish back into the stream. As we finished fishing, Mom called us for breakfast. I stepped into camp, and Mom handed me a pot and told me to go to the stream and fill it with water.

As I knelt next to the stream to fill the bucket, Uncle Jimmy came up beside me. "See that?" he asked.

"What" I responded, leaning further down towards the place his finger pointed to.

Before I knew what was happening, I was reeling head-first into the stream. As I came up gasping in response to the early morning chill of the water, I saw Uncle Jimmy bent over laughing.

Scrambling back onto land, I glared at him before filling the pot with water while keeping an eye on him to avoid another unwanted wash in the stream.

That afternoon, we congregated in an area where the water pooled. Laying on a flat rock dotting the perimeter, I warmed my skin before jumping into the refreshing pool. Dog paddling in a deep area, I was unpleasantly surprised by a nibble on my pinky toe. A large fish mistook me for food and latched on before being quickly kicked off by my panicked response. The reality of the monstrous-sized fish that called this pond home caused me to retreat to the shallow water.

"Come on, Jimmy," Harry called out.

Sitting up, Jimmy looked quizzically at Harry.

To my surprise, Harry lifted me onto his shoulders before calling Charlene over and then calling out to Jimmy again, "Grab that ball and come in."

Jimmy grabbed a beach ball that had no owner. It had been bobbing near us in the water for a while. Jimmy got the idea and jumped in the water, hoisting Charlene onto his shoulders as we tossed the ball back and forth.

I was athletic and competitive, so I wanted to play chicken fights. My sister had a sweet disposition, which did not lend her the competitive edge I possessed. After tossing the ball back and forth for a bit, Charlene jumped down to get warm and refresh herself.

"You want to play chicken?" Harry asked.

"Yes." I grinned down at him from my spot on his shoulders.

Throwing me up into the air, I flew up and then smacked down into the water. I came up laughing.

Mom came over, got on Harry's shoulders, and pointed me to Uncle Jimmy.

I swam over and jumped on his shoulders as Harry grinned at me. "Now we can play chicken."

I put up a good fight but inevitably got knocked off a few times before deciding I was tired and needed to get warm. I wish I could say I was a gracious loser, but I wasn't. My parents chuckled to themselves as I quickly departed, face downcast.

We spent the week swimming and hiking and explored areas off the beaten path. Mom also taught me about different plants and their medicinal uses. She patiently pointed out poisonous berries and cautioned my sister and me against eating from plants even though there were many from which you could eat. Bepop showed me how to whittle a stick of wood and create something out of it. We roasted marshmallows and sipped hot cocoa in the evenings after dinner. All too soon, our first vacation ended. Yet, the connections created on that trip were priceless.

This was the first of many camping trips and adventures we would embark upon as a family. It solidified my acceptance of Harry as a member of our tribe. Though I still missed my dad greatly and vacillated between resentment and excitement about Harry's presence in our family. Like the little bits of wood falling off the whittling stick, my resolve to dislike him slowly chipped away.

REFLECTION

Grooming Steps Two and Three (continued): Gain the Trust of the Victim and the Family Fact: Harry spent over two years earning the trust of Andrea and her family before any abuse happened. Many chapters will portray average family experiences, illustrating steps two and three of grooming.

Enriching Family Experiences
This was the first family vacation in Andrea's family. The perception was that Harry being part of the family allowed them to have a vacation.

7

TWO SEASONS IN UTAH

Back for only a few days, Harry and Mom called a family meeting and announced we were moving to Utah. Still basking in the glow of the redwood trees and the lights of Las Vegas, my sister and I were very receptive to the idea. Within a week, we packed up our apartment, sold or discarded all unnecessary items, and off we went.

Once again, we packed up a cooler full of food and drinks and said goodbye to our grandparents, this time for good. It felt surreal to know we would soon live in a place without them right around the corner. Harry's brother lived in Ogden, and we would stay with him and his family until we got a place of our own. Meeting new cousins felt like an exciting new prospect, and it kept the anxiety of leaving the familiar at bay. I didn't really have any close friends or attachments I left behind other than my extended family. In this respect, my sister followed my lead, so we collectively set our minds and hearts on what lay ahead.

Traveling with two new kittens proved to be a stellar experience. Our travel pace plodded along, hitting rest stops along the way.

Hopping out at one of these stops, Mom called out, "Don't let the kittens wander," just as one ran up a tree. "Climb up there and get it," she said while staring up at the tree trunk.

I liked tree climbing, but there were not enough low branches to grasp, to get to where the cat was. Harry had to climb the tree to get Mabel so we could leave. Our trip was enjoyable, and that was arguably the biggest challenge we encountered.

The scenery massaged the senses. San Diego has slight changes for each season, and our mountains are small. Our travels brought majestic mountains made of jagged rock towering high above us. We encountered a fair share of animals too.

"Look," Charlene squealed as a herd of elk occupied the road in front of us. We had never seen so many animals on the roadway at once before.

It was raining heavily when we arrived in Ogden, Utah. Even the rain felt different in this new place. When it rains in California, the raindrops are thin and light, so you get a slight sheen on you running from your house to the car. In Utah, the drops are the size of bullets, and you get soaked.

Charlene and I watched in wonder as we pulled up in front of our cousin's house. This sight will be imprinted in my memory for the rest of my life. Arriving there felt like stepping into a different time. The whole family, dog and cat included, sat on their huge front porch, watching the lightning and thunder as the buckets of rain poured heavily onto the hungry ground around their house. The weedy earth drank it in. The house itself resembled the Amityville home in its worn-down state of being. The paint of the huge two-story Victorian was steadily chipping away. Darkened windows loomed over us, letting us know who was boss.

We got drenched while exiting the car and running up onto the porch. Candy, their St. Bernard, a bit intimidating due to her size, greeted us, but she was sweet and harmless.

Aside from the slobber, I really liked her. The cat, Snoops, was indifferent to us, but much to the kittens' distaste, he was quite interested in them. We all plopped down on the porch and watched the rainstorm together. As the lighting and thunder waned, introductions were made, and our entourage wiped our feet on the threadbare doormat and headed into the slightly formidable house.

I asked to use the bathroom, and my cousin Peggy locked arms with me and led me up the stairs. Pulling the door open, she exclaimed, "Oh, you are going to have to wait a minute; somebody beat you to it."

Looking over her shoulder, I saw Snoops, the cat occupying the toilet. If a cat could frown, he would have been doing it. He did not appreciate being disturbed.

Looking at Peggy, I burst into laughter before asking, "How did you teach a cat to use a toilet?" I kept waiting for someone from *America's Funniest Home Videos* to pop out of the hallway and film the event.

Peggy just shrugged her shoulders," I don't know. It's a mystery I guess."

"You kids get the table set for dinner." Aunt Pamela walked into the kitchen as she spoke. Peggy and Buddy brought plates and glasses out and began directing their younger siblings, Gemma, and Timmy, to place them around the table.

"You can sit next to me." Gemma beamed up at Charlene.

We sat down when Aunt Pamela and Uncle Buck came to the table. Soup with warm rolls was our entrée. It was a comforting meal with the rain drumming outside. We made small talk, answering questions about our trip and asking our cousins what they liked to do for fun. Aunt Pamela and Mom began getting to know each other. Uncle Buck didn't pay much attention to us kids. He was wrapped up in conversation with Harry, making plans to go house hunting. Soon, we felt the effects of the long trip, and off to bed we all went.

The first week with our new cousins was full of fun adventures. The neighborhood had extensive rural areas, and we explored them all. The trees in Ogden were lush and colorful in the early summertime as opposed to stick trees in the winter, and this summer was no exception. Large maples boasted leaves that beamed with beautiful rusts and oranges. They were the shining crown on a town that appeared as though it had not changed in fifty years even though we had just arrived. There was a feel to it, similar to watching a black-and-white film. As we passed the back door of a bar that resided along the railroad tracks, my cousin knocked on the back door and asked for some peanuts. To my surprise and awe, they gave us two bags and sent us on our way. Munching on our peanuts, Peggy, Buddy, and I trudged along the river's edge.

Once we arrived at our desired destination, we set out exploring. Peggy and I sat on some rocks, enjoying the sunshine.

"Hey Andrea, come over here," shouted Buddy from half a football field down the river.

I joyfully skipped down to where he was crouched down, picking through the rocks that pooled in this area.

"Here, help me out," he said.

When I just stared blankly at my cousin, he scolded me. "Well, if you want to skip rocks, you need to find some good ones."

"Skip Rocks? What is that?" I responded.

"What kind of girl ain't never skipped rocks before?" he asked, staring at me with a look that said city girl all over it.

"You gotta get the flat ones like this," he explained as he proudly displayed a nice smooth rock in his palm that looked like it belonged there.

Buddy stood up and turned his body sideways as he masterfully flung the rock across the still river. It glided across the top of the water, breaking the perfect reflection, and hopped five times before giving way to gravity and disappearing into the slightly murky water.

My face lit up with fascination as I said, "Let me try." I quickly found a handful of rocks and showed my cousin.

He picked through them, throwing them back down to the ground, speaking curses on them. "Too small, too heavy, not flat enough, not the right shape."

At last, we found a perfect rock for me to make my debut toss. "Here goes," I yelled as I turned sideways and flung my treasure toward to opposite side of the riverbank only to watch it pitifully sink into the water.

Buddy grinned with glee. Peggy meandered over to join us, and we spent another hour digging up the perfect bits of stone for our skips. I managed to get a three-skipper before we moved on.

We trudged towards home, crossing a footbridge that served as an overpass to the cars racing across the freeway. I watched in terror as Buddy easily catapulted his body over the unfenced hand railing and dangled over the edge of the bridge. He hung above the vehicles below, resembling a circus trapezius with no safety net. His fingers were visible on the sidewalk where he hung over the side of the footbridge and his hands moved in sync with our steps. As we walked on the sidewalk he swung his body from side to side pacing us.

"What are you doing?" I screamed as I looked helplessly over at his sister Peggy.

She looked completely uninterested. "He'll be fine. He does it all the time. If he falls, he will get what his dumb ass deserves. Buddy, get back up here!" she prodded him on my behalf.

I thought my heart would beat out of my chest. All I could think was It was a good thing Charlene didn't come with us. She would have been traumatized, and I would never have been able to go out with them again. As it stood, Buddy pulled himself back over the rail and pranced over to us like a proud peacock as we neared the end of the footbridge.

"That was so stupid. You could have been killed if you had fallen!" I glared at my cousin, feeling grateful there were no more bridges to conquer.

"It was kinda cool. You gotta admit it. I bet you don't have any brave cousins like me in California." Buddy's grin spread from ear to ear.

Summer was enchanting. We got our own place about three weeks after arriving in Ogden. It was a little cottage-style house with floral prints on the curtains, a short white picket fence, and green shrubbery lining the grass edges. I talked Mom and Harry into letting me room in the basement, which I was ecstatic about. California does not have basements, as there are no tornados, so this was a novelty to me. I felt extremely excited to have my own room. There was a door and a window from the main room in the basement leading out to the side of the house and into a small storage space. The thrill of living downstairs eventually wore off as I battled with the chill and the spiders that also accompanied rooming in the basement.

Our kittens, Mable, and Mordecai, joyfully adjusted to their new surroundings. I had a ball of yarn that they viciously chased all around the yard.

"Don't let them eat it. They'll get hairballs," Mom would chide as they tried to lick the yarn.

Summer heat kicked up, and we attached a sprinkler to the hose that moved back and forth as we ran carelessly through the water to keep cool. A steady flow of popsicles helped during the heat wave. Finding it easier to cool off when I was hot than to get warm when I was cold, I enjoyed it.

Once I got my room in order, Peggy came to spend the night. I didn't bring a lot of my posters and room decorations with me, but I had a floral bedspread and a circular rug.

Peggy and I drew pictures of flowers on cardstock and stuck them on the brick wall. She also helped me re-organize my shelves, so the things I used the most were easily accessible.

As we got comfortable in my new space, she asked, "What is there to do in California?"

"Well, we went to the zoo, and there is an aerial tram that you ride on, so you don't have to walk to the other side. It's pretty cool. They have polar bears and penguins on one side. There is a beautiful bird sanctuary that we walk through and a snake den. The last time we went, the gorillas were throwing their poop at us. They are so gross." I laughed thinking about it.

"Did you go to the beach a lot? I would go to the beach all the time if I lived there," she gushed.

"No, not all the time," I thoughtfully murmured. I shared with her how I spent a lot of time with my grandparents in the summer. "They have a community pool in their neighborhood, so I swam there a lot," I told her, feeling a little wistful at the thought of summer with my grandparents.

Peggy spoke of a boy she liked and how catty the girls were at school. I admired the way she paid no mind to people who didn't treat her with the respect she deserved. She always seemed to understand that it was their loss. It would take me years to latch on to that fact.

We ate popcorn and drank soda while we swapped our stories. As the day slipped away, darkness came, and Peggy and I changed into our pajamas. The plan was to join everybody upstairs to watch *The Twilight Zone*. We plodded up the steps upstairs to the living room. I stopped halfway up and went back to turn off the light in my bedroom. Reaching for the lamp, I screamed as Harry opened the door, entering my room from the storage area.

"What were you doing out there? How long were you out there?"

"Oh, I was looking for something for your Mom."

"I didn't hear you inside there. The outside door into the storage unit is so squeaky." I looked at Harry thoughtfully.

"You must have been too busy gabbing with your cousin. Come on." Squeezing by me, he started up the stairs.

The next day, we went back to Buck and Patsy's. Being himself, Buddy jumped off a little storage shed with an umbrella screaming, "Geronimo!" It turns out umbrellas do not slow down falls, contrary to every cartoon we had ever watched. Buddy spent the rest of that summer with a cast on his arm. We all had a few more adventures before our glorious summer ended.

Winter arrived and brought a less enchanting theme. Harry and my mom had trouble finding employment in a primarily Mormon town. We were not Mormon. In fact, we didn't even go to church. When school started, the stark difference between most of the other families in the area and us became painfully obvious. Making friends proved difficult. Many kids were not allowed to play with my sister and me, and it was no easier for my parents. My mom ended up working at a burger joint for meals, and Harry got a job at a rendering plant with his brother. It wasn't long before they couldn't afford the rent in our little cottage, and we ended up back at our cousin's house.

I cannot recall any time before or since that winter ever being that cold. The chill in the Ogden air was all-encompassing. I felt it in my bones like the grim reaper attempting to suck us in.

Shortly before we moved back into the house with our cousins, the electricity got turned off. Mom, Charlene, and I cuddled up on our couch that day, with every blanket piled on top of us. We put socks on our feet and mittens on our hands, and each of us dreaded the next trip to the bathroom.

REFLECTIONS

Grooming Step Four: Gain Access/Isolate the Victim

Moving to Utah isolated the family from everything familiar and created a reliance on Harry that was not there in California.

Trust your Instincts

Andrea questioned why she didn't hear Harry in the storage room next to the basement. The proximity was so close that if he was rustling through boxes, she and Peggy should have heard him. Harry was evasive when she questioned him about his presence there. Andrea now suspects that Harry was watching her and her cousin change their clothes.

8

CHRISTMAS BREAK AND A PLUS ONE

December quickly descended onto our doorstep, and with it came a call from our father with an invitation to visit him in San Diego during our Christmas break from school. I couldn't wait!

Exhilarating thoughts of us going to our favorite places together raced through my head as our plane flew through the sky on our flight toward San Diego. We would visit Uncle Pat and Aunt Valerie, eat breakfast at The Spice Rack, and sit under the tiny dock across Windemere Court, digging up sand crabs while Dad went for a run around the bay.

The sound of wheels rolling down the aisle interrupted my thoughts. Charlene and I turned and saw a stewardess pushing a cart down the aisle. We watched as she asked some of the other people if they wanted drinks.

"Can we have a drink?" Charlene asked me.

"I don't know. We don't have any money."

As the stewardess approached us, she said, "What can I get you girls to drink?"

"Um, We don't have any money," I shyly said to her my voice barely above a whisper.

"Oh, It's free. You don't need any money. What would you like?

"Coke please," I answered feeling relieved.

"What about you honey?" She looked over at Charlene.

"Apple juice please," she smiled as she made her request.

The stewardess came back with our drinks and bags of peanuts for us to snack on.

Charlene and I were nervous about flying alone. When we had boarded the plane, a stewardess had come to escort us, and she reassured us that she would make sure we got to our destination safely. I didn't think about food or drinks at the time.

When the plane landed our stewardess walked us off the plane to the waiting area where our Dad was waiting to meet us. Dad gave us hugs and kisses before we headed to the baggage claim area to pick up our suitcases. We had to wait for our luggage to appear on the baggage conveyor. Once we got our suitcases, we left the airport and excitedly piled into the car.

As Dad started talking, my face fell with disappointment. Dad began explaining how a *friend* had come with him, and she would be at the apartment when we got there. My overwhelming thought was, "She is going to ruin everything."

Only one other time since my parents divorced, had another woman spent time with us when we visited Dad. She was a friend of Dad's who wanted to meet my sister and me and take us to Disneyland. She was nice enough, but even as a kid, I could sense she was trying too hard to bond with us. The car ride to Disneyland was pleasant, but my father quickly rejected any suggestions or intercessions she tried to make involving us girls. It was clear we were hands-off where she was concerned. We didn't see her again. However, this time, things were different, and I knew it.

Gloria had flowing, sable hair, and sun-kissed creamy brown skin. She was from Columbia, and that first night for dinner, she prepared the best chicken and rice I have ever eaten. Though I wanted to dislike her for encroaching on my extremely limited time with Dad, I couldn't help but adore her.

Throughout our week together, we spent time attempting to understand each other. Gloria had a limited English vocabulary, and I enjoyed learning the Spanish words for every object we encountered. For example, I held up my shoe, and she said, "Zapato." We made a game of it, and it really helped to break the ice. My sister and I were both quickly enamored with her.

Dad took us to the chiropractor for an adjustment and to GNC to pick up chewable rose-hips vitamin C. He also took us shopping, and we each got a new outfit and a pair of shoes. After trying on several pairs of pants and some blouses, I had it down to two sets of clothes.

Dad gazed at me and asked, "Which one will it be?"

"I like them both," I stammered, going from one choice to the other.

"Make a choice," he stated firmly.

Though I wanted them both, I quickly made a choice, and off to the check-out line we went. This was Dad's usual practice when we visited him roughly twice a year.

Dad's consistency gave me a sense of safety and comfort. He gave us a lot of what we needed and a little bit of what we wanted. I knew what to expect when I was with him, and as I gently eased into our first week together, I felt lighter and brighter somehow. The weight of looking after my sister was no longer mine when I was with my dad. I was free to care only for myself, and the simplicity of our routine brought the security I had been missing.

Dad was not what I would call warm and fuzzy. He was direct and to the point, in stark contrast to Harry's fun and slightly mischievous demeanor. Still, there is something to be said for clear expectations.

We wrapped up our first week with Dad by visiting Aunt Val and Uncle Pat. We had an early Christmas celebration complete with a Santa Claus appearance.

"Come on, hurry," my sister cried while pulling my arm into the family room.

Our cousins, Kristin and Heather, had already claimed their spaces on the carpet adjacent to the decadently decorated tree. "Hi," Kristin waved and smiled as we entered the room.

"I want to sit by the fireplace so I won't be cold," Charlene whispered.

Waving back at Kristin, I scooched nearer to the hearth so Charlene could enjoy the light heat the fake electric logs emanated.

After fussing with gifts, Aunt Valerie hovered near the perimeter of the carpet we sat on, watching me with a keen eye. We heard a "*Ho Ho Ho*" bellowing from the garage over the light Christmas carols jingling in the background. St. Nick entered the room carrying a large bag of gifts.

As he settled on the lounge chair sweetly set in the front of the room in anticipation of his arrival, a familiar feeling began to dawn on me. Something niggling in my brain shifted, and pieces began to come together as past Christmas celebrations flew through my memory. Just as the mental picture I struggled to bring to the surface came to fruition, Aunt Valerie saw the look of recognition and snatched me up and out of the room before I could utter a word.

After the shock wore off, I blurted out, "That is Grandpa Sherman dressed up as Santa Claus."

She quickly put her finger to her lips and asked me to let it be our secret so we didn't spoil the fun for the other kids. Once she was sure I was not traumatized by the revelation and that I would comply with her oath of silence, we went back into the den. We opened a ridiculous number of gifts while sipping hot chocolate with Johnny Mathis serenading us through the newly installed surround sound.

After opening presents, we went outside to play on the backyard swing set that Santa surprised Kristin and Heather with that year. It had a slide, swings and a see saw. Charlene and I climbed the wooden steps to the upper deck so we could go down the slide. I let her go first and stayed up there eating mini marshmallows I had stuffed into my jacket pocket. The dog George came out was running in circles on the grass.

"Look at me!" Heather swung back and forth on the see-saw. Her blonde hair was flying behind her, and the swing set began to shake.

Kristin and I were the same age, and Heather and Charlene were the same age. We got along well, and we always left their house before we wanted to go. Of course, it was easy when we only got together twice a year during holidays for a couple of hours.

After our turkey feast, we piled ourselves and our gifts into Dad's station wagon and headed home, leaving behind Uncle Pat to watch football and drink his Coors Light. Aunt Val was busy cleaning up the last of the dishes.

Our time with Dad and Gloria whizzed by. Before I knew it, we packed up our little suitcases and got ready for bed. Our last evening with Dad was coming to a close, and I knew it was now or never. I finally found the courage to verbalize the question I had wanted to relay to my father all week.

As Dad tucked me neatly into bed and began to shut off the light, I latched on to his arm. "Dad," I whispered.

"Yes, Andrea, what is it?" he replied.

"Dad, I want to live with you." I barely got the words out, and if I had been standing, my little legs would have been shaking.

"I don't like it in Utah. It's really cold, and the kids at school don't like me."

Dad looked thoughtfully at me. "Well, now, you have your cousins. You like them, don't you?"

"Well, yeah, I guess," I said as I looked up at him. Truthfully, I adored my cousins, but I could feel disappointment coming my way.

Dad smiled at me as he took my hand and explained, "I am on the ship eight months out of the year. I wouldn't be home to take care of you. You need to stay with your mom. She would be sad without you."

I wanted to tell him that she wouldn't miss me because she would have Charlene, but I had mustered all the courage I had, and the moment to speak any further quickly dissipated into the night, along with my hopes.

REFLECTION

Fathers Matter

Andrea's father, David's, absence took its toll on his girls. He was a good provider, and his consistency brought a sense of security for them when he was with them. Unfortunately, it was not often enough to create the bond they needed. The lack of emotional connection with her father created a void in Andrea.

9

A FUNERAL

Charlene and I walked home from school shivering and teeth chattering. The school had become a very lonely place, and the chill of winter added to it. Nobody had played with me on the playground until recently when a boy named Armando started chasing me. Now, some of the girls were nice to me to get close to Armando, and some of the girls were even meaner to me due to the attention he showered on me.

The cold matched the landscape of my heart. My deferred desire to stay with my dad felt like a huge rejection. I had always believed I had an option about where I lived. It was a little trump card in my back pocket to play if there was ever a need for it. The reality sunk in deep that I didn't have a choice at all, and it rubbed raw on my emotions.

I didn't have long to ponder on it because we weren't home for a week when Dad called for us to go back to California. Grandma Lizzy, Grandpa Sherman's sister, had passed away. My sister and I did not spend much time with Grandma Lizzy, but I recall her being a firm, matter-of-fact woman. When I think of her, I have distinct memories of eating lunch on plates decorated with black and white specks that looked like salt and pepper. The table in her kitchen reminded me of a smaller version of the table from the *Brady Bunch* sitcom. She ran a daycare out of her home, and playpens lined her living room.

It's funny the things you remember about a person. Reflecting, it surprises me that Dad brought us back for the funeral because he didn't bring us for Grandpa Sherman's, and we were closer to him.

Grandma's service was in what I believe was a Catholic church with beautiful stained-glass windows. Afterward, with my petite hand in my father's large one, I watched him gaze contemplatively out of one of those windows for a long while. We just stood there together quietly, not speaking. I stared up at my dad with wonder. What is he thinking? How does he feel? Dad was neither a sharer nor a crier. That moment seemed like a millisecond and a thousand years passing by simultaneously. The craving to connect with my father and to know him burned inside me, though I couldn't define it.

After the funeral service and luncheon were over, we went back to Dad's. We got the privilege of being there for the weekend. Saturday night rolled around, and Uncle Paul showed up with Jason and Jordan. Uncle Paul was Dad's best friend, and his boys were the same ages as us girls. They had decided we would all take a ferry ride around the bay on the Bahia Belle.

Bundled in our winter coats, we stood on the dock together, enjoying the clear starry night. Charlene and I plotted with Jason and Jordan about ditching our dads to explore downstairs, and without a word like shots from a cannon, they both bolted down the stairs. We stood there with our mouths agape when a stench that inspired the gag reflex permeated the whole upper deck.

Confused, I began looking around, and my father looked at Uncle Paul and said, "Damn you, man. Geez, you have no class, Paul. Zero. I can't take you anywhere."

The deck cleared as people hurriedly hit the stairs to retreat below to safer airspace.

"Come on over here, girls." Dad reached out his arm, and we followed him to the other side of the now-empty upper deck to enjoy the view stench free. Peeking under Dad's arm, looking for signs of our cousins, nothing but an empty stairway and jazz music pleasantly floating up from the deck below greeted my gaze.

Uncle Paul shamelessly drank his scotch with a smile etched deeply onto his finely chiseled face and commented, "It isn't my fault they didn't want to enjoy the view."

Turning away without responding, Dad turned his attention to Charlene. "Are you getting cold? Come on, Let's head down below and get something to eat."

Looking back at Uncle Paul, he called out as we descended the stairs, "I'll feed your poor kids too while we are down there. They're ashamed to claim you."

Laughing at the table with our cousins, we enjoyed Shirley Temples with our meals which was a great novelty. By the time Uncle Paul straggled down to dinner, we were feasting on brownies with vanilla bean ice cream and hot fudge. Dad and Uncle Paul had an after-dinner cocktail before the Belle came to her final rest at the dock, and we all scampered onto the walkway and headed back to the apartment. Waving goodbye, we watched the lights in the back of their car fade away as Uncle Paul and the boys sped off down Mission Bay Drive.

REFLECTIONS

Desire for Connection

Andrea recalls a profound moment with her father at the funeral. She wanted to know what he thought and how he felt. She mentions that he was "neither a sharer nor a crier," and the emotional distance had such an impact that she carried this memory into adulthood.

10

MAKING MISCHIEF

The glamour of living in a place where there were definitive seasons was long gone when we resumed school after Christmas break. I officially hated Utah winters. To add to the misery, not long after we returned to Utah, Charlene tripped on the school stage and knocked out her two front teeth. It would be several years before her adult teeth replaced them.

The excitement of a new place had worn off for my mom as well, particularly since we no longer had our own place to live. Job prospects were grim, and Harry worked nights at the rendering plant with Uncle Buck. A cool vibe lingered between my mom and Aunt Pamela, but the lack of resources and the shared space wore on the adults. They were snappier and stricter with us kids, so we did our best to keep our Ps and Qs in line.

The weekend came, and us kids itched to get away from our parents, so we headed down the street to the Kiefer's. They had a daughter named Jamie and a son named Joey that Buddy and Peggy played with sometimes. Boy, going over there was a mistake. After a game of truth or dare got out of hand, Jamie went crying to her Mother and we found ourselves hiding from Mrs. Kiefer.

"Get down. She's coming," Buddy barked into my ear.

When Jamie went crying to her Mom, Joey went inside and the rest of us scattered. Peggy took Charlene and headed back towards her house. Gemma and Timmy couldn't get away before Mrs. Kiefer came outside so they were hiding in the bushes. Buddy and I hid in the basement.

I was never more terrified in my eight-year-old life. Peeking through the tiny vent screen of the Kiefer's basement, we watched Mrs. Kiefer, in all of her girth, striding around the side of the house, calling out to Timmy and Gemma, "I seen y'all. I know it was you kids. I am going to be talking to your mama. You can count on that."

"We shouldn't have hidden in here, Buddy," I screeched. "She is gonna find us."

"No, she ain't, and even if she did, she's too big to come down here and git us."

"Yeah, but we are still stuck down here in her basement," I snapped back at him.

"Aww, quit fussing. I hide in here every time. She ain't never caught me yet."

Mrs. Kiefer stood at the edge of her property, looking around with her eagle eye. "I had enough of this nonsense from you, and I am gonna put an end to it today. Y'all won't be allowed to play down here with Jamie and Joey no more," she bellowed.

Mrs. Kiefer was turning to go back into the house when Timmy and Gemma bolted out of the bushes, but old Mrs. Kiefer was much quicker on her feet than anybody expected. In one quick swoop, she had Gemma's arm in her hand, and she dragged her inside the house.

"Oh, man. I told them to stay put," Buddy said, even though they couldn't hear him.

"What are we going to do?" I asked in a panic.

"Well, I guess the gigs up." Buddy wiped his hand across his face. "We might as well get outta here."

"Yes." Spider webs galore surrounded us, and I was relieved to be crawling out of the basement. I knew something had crawled on my neck, and I brushed at it even though I had already done it ten times.

Staring in horror, I watched Buddy walking to their front door. "What are you doing?" I hissed.

"Well, we can't leave Gemma in there with the old bat. She's probably terrified."

"Oh my God. We are going to be in so much trouble!" I was already imagining the beating I was going to get.

"Aww, nah, we ain't. She said dare. If you don't want to do the dare and you're gonna cry, you shouldn't be playing the game." Head high, he continued, then boldly rapped on the door like he owned the place while I slowly trailed behind him.

"Well, get in here." Mrs. Kiefer grabbed onto my arm and sat me down on her quilt-covered couch right next to Gemma.

When she reached for Buddy, he pulled his arm back and retorted quickly, "Nobody puts their hands on me besides my pa."

"Well, he will if I have anything to say about it," she scolded.

He didn't respond but held her gaze steady, and she didn't test him.

The Kiefer's home was full of knick-knacks and felt overcrowded. I thought I felt a spring popping out right underneath the fabric of the worn and lumpy couch. Sitting in a stranger's house I felt oddly exposed and wrapped my arms around myself in an effort to self soothe.

Jamie Kiefer sat on a lounge chair across the room from us. She dramatically waved her hands in front of her mouth saying, "I can't get the taste out of my mouth." She was clearly putting on a show for her Mother.

Mrs. Kiefer looked from Jamie to us and said, "You kids are gonna stay right here until I can get your mother on the phone," she stated with no small amount of satisfaction.

To our delight, the phone rang and rang, but nobody answered it.

"Well, you are just going to have to wait here until they get home," she said as she plunked the phone receiver down on the base a little too loudly.

"We gotta get home. You can't keep us here. Aunt Theda told me to be home by 4:00 PM with all of the kids, and she won't be none too happy with you holding us here."

"That's fine. I will just walk you home then," Mrs. Kiefer gloated as she stood up and motioned for us to follow.

We marched home together, and I felt like I was walking the plank. None of our parents were home when we got there, but Buddy's older brother Eddie was home.

Mrs. Kiefer went on and on about how we tricked her sweet little Jamie into eating a concoction that wasn't fit for human consumption, and if we were her children, she would have paddled our behinds.

Eddie turned to Buddy with a raised voice. "Didn't I tell you to behave yourself and set an example for your cousins? Get in the house right now." He looked at us next. "All of y'all get in there now before I whoop the lot of ya."

Mrs. Kiefer departed momentarily with a satisfied look on her face. I knew Eddie planned to beat us with the hot wheel track. I sat anxiously watching Mrs. Kiefer leave as Eddie flicked his cigarette off the porch into the dirt and mounted the steps into the house.

"Well, y'all are lucky Ma and Aunt Theda aren't home. What did I tell you about playing with them sissy Kiefer kids? It ends the same every time." He looked at my frightened face, then he and Buddy chuckled up a storm. Eddie stared at me, exclaiming, "What did you think I was gonna do?

Tar and feather ya?" Turning his head to Buddy, he asked, "Where is Timmy?"

With amusement, Buddy responded, "Aww, he is probably out behind the shed waiting for Mrs. Kiefer to get by so they can come in the house."

"Well, go find them and get cleaned up before Ma and Theda get back with the groceries. Y'all look like you been rolling with hogs."

Our parents arrived shortly after this escapade. Knowing we'd dodged a bullet, I was extra helpful with dinner preparations—almost to the point of arousing suspicion.

After I offered to help for the third time, Mom looked at me and said, "What's got into you?"

After dinner, Peggy and I snuck off to her room.

"Y'all didn't need to shove that concoction into her face."

"It wasn't my fault; I didn't know he put dirt in there. I thought it was just bologna with some cinnamon and spicy sauce on it. It was a dare!" I snapped back.

"Well, we will be lucky if Mrs. Kiefer doesn't talk to your mom or mine. It wasn't nice." Peggy grimaced at me.

Looking over at Peggy I said, "She wasn't fun to play with. Why did you want to go over there anyhow?"

"I don't know, just bored, I guess. We wanted to get away from our house for a while and needed somewhere to go."

Peggy smiled as she settled into her side of our shared mattress. Wrapping ourselves in the covers, It wasn't long before we both fell fast asleep.

REFLECTIONS

Culture & Camaraderie

The culture in Utah was different, and that presented challenges for Andrea and Charlene's parents. From a predatorial standpoint, shared living quarters also reduced the opportunity for physical isolation of kids.

Living with their cousins brought built-in camaraderie for Andrea and Charlene, along with changes in family dynamics. Buddy was accustomed to caring for his younger siblings. He was not going to leave one behind to face the consequences alone.

11

FAMILY FUN & FAREWELL

Having Peggy and Buddy to pal around with made life fun—Peggy was becoming like a big sister to me, and Charlene had Gemma for companionship. We didn't always have to be together, and I felt grown up hanging out with my older cousin. It wasn't that I didn't like my sister; I did. After Dad left, I felt like I couldn't do anything on my own without her, and I resented it. It wasn't her fault, but she got the brunt of my feelings and having cousins of our respective ages gave us breaks from one another. We were able to change the dynamic of our relationship, and it felt good.

Hanging out with Peggy took some of the pressure off the weightiness I felt after vacation with Dad. I didn't have as much time to think obsessively about the disappointment and hurt I felt or roll the scene around on replay in my head.

My teacher wanted to put me into a different class due to the grade differences in the Utah school curriculum versus California, and I was nervous about the prospect of changing classes. I had always been a good student, and I felt like my teacher was disappointed with my progress which was another hit to my crumbling self-esteem.

Peggy gave me some encouragement saying, "It doesn't matter what they think. We know you're smart and good, and if they can't see that, it's their problem, not yours. Those snobby kids don't deserve to be your friend."

I admired Peggy's resolve to be herself and not mold into a more socially acceptable version of herself, and I wished I had that kind of courage. As it was, I felt left out and alone, and I would have turned my skin inside out if I thought they would accept me. Regardless, Peggy helped me with homework in the subjects I wrestled with and kept a constant infusion of pep talks coming my way. She wasn't liked any more than I was—she just cared less. We understood each other, and Peggy was my safe place. She never told anybody anything I shared with her, and she never judged me.

The weekend arrived, and we got an unexpected surprise: Harry took Friday night off of work, and Mom had the day off on Saturday. Mom ushered Charlene and me up early saying, "Get dressed, sleepyheads. Breakfast is waiting." Donuts and milk were on the table. We ate quickly and gulped down our milk before our parents told us to get ready to go.

"Let's go," Harry trilled as he opened the front door to a shining sun. "Hurry up. The snow will melt before we get there." He laughed at the absurdity of his statement. (It would take three days for the snow to melt, even with warm days.)

Piling into the car with our hats, mittens, and thermal leggings under our pants, we met up with our cousins and rode to the mountains to go tubing. After an hour and fifteen minutes on the road, we pulled into a parking lot that had been snow plowed. We gathered our tubes and began walking across the street towards a large snow-covered hill.

Growing up in Southern California, Charlene and I had no experience with snow tubing. The only snow we had seen was in Julian, and it was just enough to make snowballs and play for an afternoon. The first step made it clear that this was much deeper and denser than the snow we had experienced.

Slow in climbing to higher ground, I was almost flattened when Buddy flew down the hill in his huge inner tube.

"Stay off the track," Mom said, pulling me aside.

"What track?" I asked. All I saw was white in every direction.

Mom pointed out a slight indentation in the snow where previous tubes had slid down the hill. It was difficult to see if you were not looking for it. Once we reached the top of the hill, Mom got inside a tube, put Charlene on her lap, and off they went. Their laughter echoed as they soared to the bottom. It wasn't long before I was flying down the hill in my tube. The experience was exhilarating. With renewed energy, I raced my cousin back to the top of the hill to do it again.

Soaring back down the track, we tried to bump each other off our tubes. We kept it up until we were too exhausted to walk up the hill anymore.

Gathering back at the car, Mom served us hot cocoa in some Styrofoam cups. Once our insides were warmed, we peeled off some layers of clothing and got cozy in the car for the ride home.

Entertaining ourselves, we sang songs as our car rolled down the highway. "99 bottles of beer on the wall, 99 bottles of beer, you take one down and pass it around, 98 bottles of beer on the wall." We sang until our parents couldn't stand it anymore and then moved on to the next crazy car song.

Even though things were challenging in Utah, life was simple. There is something to be said about a day of tubing with your family, car songs, and cocoa. These are the things that ground me when life's pressures feel heavy. I hope I never underestimate the worth of a timely word or a hug. My prayer is that I have imparted these values to my children and they count people as more worthy than things. Most of all, may they understand that they are perfectly perfect just as they are. Just them. They are the greatest of my life's treasures.

I have never gone hungry a day in my life, but my parents did at times that year we spent in Ogden. Though it was sometimes imperfect, I am forever grateful for my parents' care. The sacrifices they made are not lost on me. Someone once said that what does not kill you makes you stronger, and in this case, it proved true. That year bonded us together as a family in an unexpected way. My perception of Harry changed immensely. The hard truth that I would not be living with my dad was a bitter pill to swallow, and though he was not my dad, Harry made our family dynamic flow in a way that benefited all of us.

There was a time during our stay in Utah when I heard Harry and Mom discussing the possibility of sending my sister and me to my grandparents until they could get on their feet, and I had feared it would happen. They did everything they could to keep us together.

Since my Mom and Dad's divorce, there was tension between my mom and me. During this season of life, it felt like we created an unspoken agreement—we were doing this together, and the tension between us lessened.

This pattern would continue for many years, almost like an instinctive survival mechanism. Harry became a buffer between us, and from my perspective, that fact made him an invaluable part of our family. Even with the lack we experienced that year, his unfailing sense of humor and lightheartedness kept hope and fun ever-present, holding the darkness at bay.

Winter lasted forever, but once Spring hit, everything accelerated. Spring bounced into Summer, and Summer brought the end of the school year. Next came the opportunity to go back home to California. Harry's grandfather could no longer live alone in his isolated home out in the desert in a tiny blip on the map called Live Oak Springs. Grandma and Grandpa had decided to move there to care for him. That left their home in La Mesa available for occupation and provided just the respite Mom and Harry needed.

We tearfully said our goodbyes and rode west into the sunset.

REFLECTIONS

"Call it a clan, call it a network, call it a tribe, call it a family. Whatever you call it, whoever you are, you need one."—Jane Howard

Fun Fact: Peggy and Andrea are still friends.

12

NEW KIDS ON THE BLOCK

I was impressed as we traipsed into our new home—after the struggles we endured in Utah, this felt like the Ritz Carlton. We plopped our things onto the floor in the living room and ran to explore the house.

Racing Charlene down the hall, I called out, "Which room is ours?"

After some discussion, we got the room with the tile flooring. I was happy because I didn't have to worry about tracking dirt onto the carpet. There were three bedrooms and a bathroom down that hallway. Unfortunately, Grandpa's office remained in one of the rooms, and nobody was allowed to go inside.

The garage had been converted into a day room with a door leading into the kitchen. It was bright and spacious with crisp, white curtains over the small window above the sink facing the front of the house parallel to the front door. Tile ending and carpet beginning separated the kitchen and living room. A sliding glass door led onto the backyard patio and provided a view of the planter boxes with flowers. They were placed under an awning that covered the patio alongside lemon trees with ripening, fragrant fruit. A beautiful bird of paradise was blooming; however, the crown jewel of this house was the pool.

Walking past the concrete patio, I stood in awe, staring at the peanut-shaped pool. I thought, "Wow, we live in a house with a pool." I immediately began dreaming about my summer of swimming and sunshine. I imagined playing Marco Polo and swimming until my toes were so wrinkled they might fall off. I could already smell the Coppertone on my skin.

We spent a few weeks unpacking and settling in. I organized my side of the room. I had a fair collection of Nancy Drew novels, a few Hardy Boys books, and some new poetry books and journals I wanted to keep close. The other reading materials could stay boxed in the closet until it was their time to shine. My dresser displayed my jacks, a diary, and the pink box that encased my record player that used 45-inch records. I had a good collection of songs that accompanied classic Disney stories—Cinderella was a favorite. One non-Disney record I had told the story of the Three Billy Goats Gruff. I listened to those records over and over, and even though I had gotten the record player when I was much younger, I still cherished it.

After unpacking some board games and finding places on my shelf for them to reside, the day grew warm, and I longed to get out of my stuffy room. Since I hadn't been to school, and we had been there such a brief time, I didn't have any friends yet, so I put on my bathing suit and jumped in the pool. I swam around a bit and then went out front to practice cartwheels and back bends on the lawn. Unbeknownst to me, I was about to meet one of the most influential people in my life.

I was turning cartwheels in the yard when a boy came racing up the street. Another boy with glasses and sun-kissed light brown hair was right behind him and caught up to him right on my front lawn. He tossed his glasses on the grass near the bushes and immediately began punching the other boy and rolling all over the ground.

Racing into the house, I yelled, "Harry, help. Come here quick."

Harry came outside and stood, arms crossed, looking amused as he watched them beat each other to a pulp.

Hearing the ruckus, Mom came outside and looked at Harry unamused before commanding, "Make them stop."

"Ok, ok, knock it off," Harry said lazily as he walked slowly towards the boys, who finally got up and dusted themselves off. "Where do you kids live?"

They pointed to a house catty corner from ours.

"You are supposed to be helping me unpack," the older one said to the younger one as he picked up his glasses from the ground where he had thrown them.

I had been steered into the house by my mom when she saw the boys fighting, so I eavesdropped through the screen door, watching as they headed back to their house while my mom scolded Harry for not stopping them sooner.

"Come inside and let's set the table for dinner," said Mom as she gently put her arm over my shoulder, leading me into the kitchen while closing the front door with her other hand.

Licking my fingers, I polished off my plate of pork chops with applesauce and green beans. With Mom making coffee and Harry in the restroom, I quietly reached over and grabbed a large handful of green beans from Charlene's plate and put them on my own. To say that Charlene hated green beans would be the understatement of the year. I knew she would not be excused and would sit at the table until midnight if she didn't finish everything on her plate. She smiled gratefully at me and shoved the few beans left on her plate into her mouth with a spoonful of applesauce, trying not to gag.

I was delighted to find out we had peach pie à la mode for dessert. After greedily eating two pieces of pie, I reluctantly conceded that it was time to clean up. Charlene cleared the table, and I washed the dishes. Grandma's house had a dishwasher, but my parents were not inclined to use it. Dishes were to be washed, dried, and put away. Nothing was left lingering on the countertop.

Mom and Harry said Charlene could let them drip dry before she put them away so that we could play a board game. I wanted to play Yahtzee, but I got out-voted, so I ran to my newly organized room and picked the game of Sorry off the shelf.

We had been there for only a few weeks, but the longing for Utah had already faded into the past. Of course, our cousins had made beautiful marks on our hearts, and life was a bit lonely without them, but there was an ease about our parents that wasn't there in Utah. Mom put her Janis Joplin album on the stereo while we chose our pieces for the board game.

I sang, "Come on, come on, come on and take it," as I put my red pieces on the board.

REFLECTIONS

New Beginnings

After the employment, social and financial challenges the family faced in Utah, this seemed like the fresh start everyone needed. Harry's true colors would be revealed in this place.

13
LEMONS, FOOTBALL, & FANGS

"Hey, what's your name?" asked a tan teenager walking by my house as I sat on the grass eating a lemon with salt on it.

"Andrea," I responded shyly, looking up.

"You got any more of those lemons," he inquired with a smile.

"Yes, we have lemon trees in the backyard."

"Will you go get me one?"

"Ok," I said, jumping up.

"And get some sugar too," he called out as I walked through the front door and headed through the house to the backyard.

"Sugar?" I paused and yelled back, "You eat lemons with salt!"

After returning with two lemons, sugar, and salt, the boy sat down on the curb with me and said, "I'm Danny," as he began to sprinkle sugar on the lemons. "Try it like this. It's better than salt." He handed me a lemon slice with sugar on it while asking, "Do you have any brothers?"

"No, just a little sister and me. Why?"

"Everybody's going to play football in about ten minutes," he said, looking across the street.

"Oh. Can girls play?"

"You want to play football?" he asked.

"I don't really know how to play," I wavered.

"We'll teach you."

"Let me go ask my parents if I can play," I yelled, excitedly running into the house. I had met a couple of the neighborhood kids already. The Horton's lived across the street, and so did the Sanders who had a son named Sam, who was much older than me—he drove already—and their daughter, Lira, who was Charlene's age. Bobby Horton was my age. He had two older brothers, David and Chuck. Andy and Matt Jones were the ones fighting each other in our front yard. They were the two youngest of the Jones family's eight kids. I still didn't have anybody my age that I could call a friend. I was bored, so I was pretty excited at the prospect of playing football, though nervous since I didn't know how to play.

When I sprung perkily into the living room, Harry was reclining in a lounge chair, smoking a cigarette, and reading a sci-fi paperback titled *Dune*.

"Can I play football with some kids outside?"

"What kids?" Harry asked, laying his book down on his lap.

"Ummm, I don't know. Danny said everybody is going to play football," I stammered.

"Who is Danny?"

"Uh, the kid outside," I said, suddenly feeling a bit unprepared for this conversation.

Harry got up, went outside, and observed Danny sitting on the grass with the lemons, salt, and sugar. "How are you doing?" he said, approaching Danny with his hand held out.

"Oh, I'm good, man," Danny responded, jumping up to shake Harry's hand.

"What is this about a football game?" Harry asked just as a group of kids converged onto the street in front of our house.

Matt, Andy, their brother Steve, Scott Hudson, and a boy named Max began tossing the football around. Soon, a kid named Todd and Chuck Horton joined in. Danny introduced Harry and me to everybody, and they showed me how to hold the football.

Mom brought out a cooler with drinks and set it down on the sidewalk. Our street sloped down in both directions, with our house in the center, so the game proceeded in front of our house.

We divided into two teams, and my sister and I got to play. Some plays were specifically set up so that we had a chance to participate. Though I realized this, I didn't mind—I was simply happy to be included. Age seemed irrelevant. My sister was the youngest at six years old, and Harry was the oldest at thirty-something.

Playing football that day was the beginning of something special. This neighborhood had a real sense of community, and we got to be a part of it. You can have manicured lawns, beautiful flower beds, and HOAs that make your neighborhood reflect perfection, yet not know any of your neighbors.

Not long after the day of the football game, my parents decided to have a pool party. Many of the people from the football game showed up at our house as well as other friends of my mom and Harry.

Bob Dylan was playing in the background, languishing at life's misfortunes blowing in the wind. Those days, you listened to a whole album before moving on to the next set of songs—there were no streaming, internet, or computers in the classrooms or for home use. After Bob Dylan, Neil Diamond got his turn, and then Kris Kristofferson.

People were diving onto a floating raft in the pool, which turned into a beachball volleyball game I thoroughly enjoyed. The BBQ steadily churned out burgers and dogs. Coolers of beer and soda were consumed, and my parents' friends doted on my sister and me.

As the sun set, the temperature dropped, and people congregated in the house. Steve went across the street to his house, then came back with his guitar. My mom got out her mandolin and Harry his clarinet, and soon a jam session started.

Seeing me ogling the instruments, Steve asked, "Do you want to play?"

"Yes," I eagerly responded as I sat on the shag carpet next to him.

He placed the guitar carefully into my lap and showed me how to properly place my fingers on the strings, wrapping my hand around the neck. I learned how to play three chords that day—D, A-minor, and G, with the end goal of learning to play *Country Roads* by John Denver.

Once I had a few chords down, Mom tried to get me to sing. Looking at me, she said, "Sing the song while you play so we can know if you are playing the right chord."

"I can't." I felt my face turning red with embarrassment at the prospect of singing in front of people.

After my refusal, Mom sent Charlene and me to take baths. Harry's sister was picking up Charlene to sleep over at their house. They had a daughter the same age as Charlene, and they were becoming friends.

Charlene got picked up, and Mom said I had to go to bed. I reluctantly left the party and my guitar strumming behind. "It's not even dark yet," I chided. "It's only seven."

"Go," Mom said, looking at me sharply. As I slowly walked down the hallway, Mom added, "You can read if you want to since it's Saturday. Just don't stay up too late."

Crawling into bed, a bright idea crossed my mind. My mom loved scary movies and books, and I had seen *Salem's Lot* by Stephen King lying in the hall closet with other things that had not yet found their way to a permanent place since the move. It can't be that scary, I thought. We were allowed to watch *Twilight Zone,* and it wasn't scary. Besides, I was eight already, almost double digits. Grabbing the book, I crawled into bed and began to read.

Some people stayed late, and some never went home. Musical notes, laughter, and the smell that I didn't know at the time was the scent of marijuana wafted down the hallway. Mom didn't bother to check if I had gone to sleep like she usually did. I read for what seemed like hours, engrossed in the characters of the book. As the plot grew, so did my anxiety. In an instant, the curiosity and thrill of doing something forbidden departed.

The shadows outside the window loomed in as I began to imagine seeing movement, and unfamiliar sounds and creaks echoed in my ears. It was eerily quiet as I suddenly realized that the music and laughter were no more. Fear gripped me. Feeling paralyzed, I struggled to get enough courage to sit up in bed and threw the book across the room into the partially opened closet door.

My heart raced, and the sound of my breathing frightened me. I wanted to get my mom, but I knew I would get in trouble for reading the book, so I stayed in bed, terrified that a cold dead hand was going to grab a hold of me any minute. *Creak* went the hinges on the bedroom door. I froze under the covers shaking and unconsciously holding my breath. The blankets lifted off of me. I sat up, jumped back, and screamed before I recognized the face in front of me.

Harry's hand bolted across my mouth and his eyes locked with mine. "Shhhhh." His hushed voice permeated the room. "Do you want to wake the whole house?"

Harry sat with his hand over my face for an abnormally long time. Sitting down on the bed, he moved his face really close to mine before removing his hand from my lips. He reached his hand up and brushed my hair back off of my cheek.

The scare had elevated my heart rate. Once the realization registered in my brain that it was only Harry and I was safe, my breathing slowed, but as I sat there with Harry, a new discomfort began to rise in me. As Harry sat there wordlessly staring at me, I felt my mouth go dry, and my palms get sweaty.

"What's going on? Did I hear a scream? Are you okay?"

Sitting up straight, Harry turned to Mom and said, "I came to check on her because the light was still on. She had a flashlight under the covers. I guess I scared her when I lifted the covers to turn it off."

Mom came over and straightened my covers. "I said you could read, not conduct a midnight vigil. Get to sleep now." As Mom bent down and kissed my forehead, Harry slid out of the room.

Hours passed before my heavy lids finally closed, and I fell into a troubled sleep. I dreamt of Harry sitting on my bed with his face close to mine, and then he opened his mouth, and fangs appeared. Just as he went to bite my neck, I woke up in a sweat.

REFLECTIONS

If it walks like a duck, looks like a duck, and quacks like a duck . . . It's a duck.

This was the first time Harry displayed questionable behavior that was obviously intentional. Unlike hiding in the connecting basement room this was more blatant. Looking back, the fact that he was under the influence may have emboldened him to come into Andrea's room. Theda unknowingly interrupted whatever ill intentions he may have had.

14

IN THE RHYTHM

Summer seemed to last forever. Time was encapsulated as if it was the molasses from a maple tree gracefully dripping and oozing down its mottled trunk in its sweet time. So naturally, I was in a hurry for it to end so I could begin school and make friends.

Mom and Harry had quickly bonded with several members of the Jones family through the love of music, camping, and a common desire to oppose governmental authority. They all also possessed a zesty appreciation and love of life, doing it on their terms, and they were creative about it.

One Friday night, we banded into teams of three and started a game of RISK that went on for 48 hours. When Charlene and I had to head to bed, the game continued without us. Jumping up in the morning to see if our respective teams were winning, we ran out to find people strewn across the living room floor and the smells of coffee and bacon frying whirling through the air most deliciously. Peeking into the kitchen like flies to food, my sister and I were spotted by Mom, who immediately put us to work.

"Go set paper plates and cups on the patio table," Mom directed. "Here, put the juice out, too," she stated, handing me a gallon of orange juice. Coffee mugs and a carton of half and half went onto the table next to the sugar bowl.

Our indoor kitchen table was a picnic table with benches with a collage of family pictures lacquered onto the tabletop, another of my mom's artistic stylings on display. We put a lot of heart into that project, and I felt a sense of pride each time I sat at that table with all the sweet memories in front of me. There were pictures of our Yosemite trip, us in Utah holding our kittens in the front yard of that little white picket-fenced house, and more recent pics from an afternoon playing hide-n-seek at Presidio Park. Seeing the pieces of our time together as a family at every meal planted hope in my heart. It made it easier to put aside the doubts about Harry's character that his recent behavior inspired.

As the bodies began to rise, people took turns sliding into the restroom to freshen up before grabbing plates of food and scattering to the randomly placed fold-out chairs or the backyard table to eat. Friends who had gone home returned and reached for coffee, and others leaned toward cans of beer to soothe their hangovers. Soon enough, everybody was fed and refreshed, and the game began again.

We played all day with different people who rotated in and out of their respective teams. Late afternoon approached, and everybody was hungry. We headed to Bob's Big Boy.

The waitress approached as we got seated in a booth large enough for our party. "I am going to have to ask you not to do that," she said, looking at a guy named Drew and one of the Jones. "Not only are you disturbing our other guests, but I am going to have to clean the window outside at the end of my shift."

Apparently, they were smushing their faces up against the windows outside, and the guests that were seated in the booths viewing this did not appreciate it.

"Oh, we're sorry. We were just messing around. We can go clean the windows for you," Scott said, trying to be charming.

"No. Thank you. What can I get you to eat?" With a pasted-on smile, she took our orders.

Charlene and I ordered waffles with strawberries. Our crew continued to laugh and razz the waitress a little bit. Somebody asked her on a date which she declined, stating, "As appealing as that sounds, I'm afraid I can't. I am washing my hair that night."

Our order came, and the whipped cream was piled high on my waffles.

"Can I have some of that?" Andy asked with his finger poised over my waffles.

"Just a little bit," I answered, guarding my plate.

Andy swiped his Shrek-sized finger over the top of my waffles and then *splat*. Cream with bits of strawberry covered Drew's face. Mayhem ensued, with food flying and even some drinks.

Charlene and I ducked down under the table. I tried to save my food, but it was a fruitless effort.

"I am going to have to ask you to leave." The store manager stood in front of our booth. Our waitress waited by the door holding it open. Once everyone in our group was out, she locked the door.

Standing outside, I complained to Mom, "I'm hungry. I didn't even get to eat my food."

"Me neither," Charlene chimed in.

"I will make you some waffles at home. Let's go, Harry." Mom started walking towards the car.

Back at home, Andy helped cook waffles, and then it was bedtime.

Drew was loosely related to the Jones clan, and it came up in conversation that he needed a place to stay. Since both of my parents had decided to enroll in barber college, the extra income would be welcomed, so the day room was converted into Drew's bedroom.

Soon, summer ended, and the more responsible rhythm of elementary school and barber college grabbed hold of our family. Busy getting her ducks in a row before all of that began, Mom had recruited Carrie to watch my sister and me for a couple of hours after school to help us with our homework and get dinner started. That would give her and Harry time to commute home and jump into the weekday routine. Carrie had taken care of us one evening during summer so that Mom and Harry could go out—she was keen to make easy bucks hanging out with us.

The easy gait that developed between Mom and me in Utah slowly developed strain. One late afternoon after a rough day at barber college, Mom came home and began barking commands. "Andrea, why is this bathroom such a mess? I thought you told me that you cleaned it."

"I did!" I retorted. "But that was on Saturday, and it got dirty again. It's Tuesday," I added.

"Don't get smart with me!" Mom's voice escalated with each word. Walking into her room, she grabbed a belt and came down the hall swinging it at me. "You don't listen to a word I say. Why don't you ever do what you are supposed to do?" With each word, the belt cracked across my skin.

As I stood there half-dressed cowering in front of my Mom, Harry came walking down the hall and stopped short in the doorway. Observing my tears and the welts on my legs, he gently put his arms around my mom's shoulders and turned her towards their bedroom. She began crying, and he quietly directed me to go to my room.

Harry interceding on behalf of my sister and I became a part of our family dynamic. The steady command of his emotions directly opposed my mother's emotional rises and falls.

This wasn't the first time, nor would it be the last time the punishment did not seem to fit the crime. Being on the end of a swinging belt as a kid was common growing up. The truth is that we repeat the behavior taught to us. I am not justifying nor excusing this action—I'm just acknowledging that I know where it came from.

As school progressed, I made friends. One late afternoon the phone rang, and it was for me. Excitedly, I put the phone receiver down on the desk and asked if I could go to Tia's house after school on Wednesday. It was a short day, and she invited me to come over and play.

My emotion welled as I was told I could go if I took my sister with me. "Tia doesn't want to play with Charlene; she wants to play with me," I wailed, unable to keep myself in check. "Why do I always have to take care of her? It isn't fair. I don't get to go anywhere without her."

"She is your sister," my mom calmly stated, unaffected by my outburst.

"So, I am never going to get to go anywhere by myself because I have a sister?" I spouted out, looking at my feet, trying to hold in the tears of frustration I was feeling.

"You get to do plenty of things by yourself," Mom answered. "If you want to go, you have to take your sister with you, and that is final."

I gave Harry a beseeching look, and as he started to speak to Mom, she repeated, "That is final, Andrea."

Harry gave me a sideways glance letting me know he was sorry, but there was nothing he could do.

I walked back to the phone and picked it up, trying to keep my voice from cracking as I dejectedly spoke, "I can only come if I bring my sister."

To my shock, Tia said, "That's great. I have a next-door neighbor her age, and she always wants to play with me. We can ask her over, and we can all have fun together."

Wednesday arrived, and after school, we all met on the playground and walked out the back gate of the school. But instead of walking directly up my street, we headed south on Lake Adlon to Tia's house. Upon arriving, we broke out the chalk, drew hopscotch squares on the sidewalk in front of her house, and began hopping through them.

Tia's mom, Shelly, was very welcoming and made snacks for us. Tia grabbed the snacks and juice boxes but ushered her mom away from us, embarrassed at the intrusion. Her neighbor came over with cabbage patch kid dolls, and we got art supplies out for her and Charlene to draw while Tia and I went into the garage and crank-called random numbers. "Is your refrigerator running?" we asked. "Well, you better go catch it," we responded, laughing, before we hung up and dialed another random number.

Tia's brother, Jace, came home just before we left, swinging his yo-yo around, bragging he could go around the world and that he was learning to walk the dog. Tia asked if we could try and got a vehement no in response. Jace smirked at us before turning briskly and stomping into the house. That day started the beginning of a friendship that would carry me through most of my elementary school years and even come to visit some of my adult days.

REFLECTIONS

Discipline vs. Punishment

Pamela Li, MS, MBA, contrasts the difference between discipline and punishment in an article titled "Discipline vs Punishment: The Difference In Child Development."[4] Dis-

---

[4]   Pamela Li, "Discipline vs Punishment: The Difference in Child Development," Parenting For Brain, October 18,

cipline helps modify behavior, develop character, and protect mental health. Punishment brings shame, is fear-based, and instills suffering for past behavior.

Many people who grow up with abuse need help to learn healthy, effective parenting skills. Some fail to discipline out of fear of repeating bad cycles, and others are still stuck.

2022, https://www.parentingforbrain.com/discipline-vs-punishment/#:~:text=The%20main%20difference%20between%20discipline%20and%20punishment%20is,parenting.%20It%20can%20be%20frustrating%2C%20discouraging%20and%20exhausting.

15

MONIQUE MAKES THREE

My friendship with Tia felt natural and blossomed quickly, so it didn't take long before we spent as much of our free time together as possible. She introduced me to Monique, and all three of us went trick-or-treating on Halloween. Since we had such a fun time, as Thanksgiving break approached, we began plotting how we could hang out together.

Harry's sister lived a few blocks from us, and she and her husband had two children, Tara and Toby. Tara and Charlene were the same age, and they invited Charlene to spend a few days at their house during Thanksgiving week. They planned to come to our house for Thanksgiving, so Charlene would come home on Thursday. This was a perfect opportunity to have a sleepover with Tia and Monique.

On Monday, Harry's sister came and picked up Charlene. That afternoon, Tia's mom, Shelly, hesitantly agreed that Tia could sleep over at our house but only because Monique would be there too. I had spent the night at Tia's, but until then, she hadn't spent the night at mine because she said her mom didn't like her to sleep over at other people's houses very much. So, after meeting my parents and chatting for a bit,

Shelly left Tia and Monique at our house with their sleeping bags and overnight gear.

We headed outside to play and found that my neighbor Matt had erected a huge ramp in the street. Four kids laid in front of the ramp. I watched with mixed feelings of horror and amusement as he rode his bike for about two house lengths to give him room to work up speed and then turned around, pedaling like crazy before whizzing over the ramp. He cleared over the kids with room to spare.

Seeing us watching him, Matt called out, "Come on, you guys. I need three more bodies."

"No way," I answered.

"I'll do it," Monique said as she walked toward the ramp. "But I want to be closest to the ramp. I'm not going way out there," she said, pointing to the kid furthest from the ramp.

Tia and I looked at each other as Monique motioned to us and yelled, "Come on."

We walked over and took our places next to Monique, arguing about who would be farthest away from the ramp. We did rock, paper, scissors because nobody had a coin to flip.

I lost, so I looked at Matt before taking my spot on the road next to Tia and said, "You better not run me over."

"I won't," he answered, displaying his slightly mischievous, dimpled smile.

The boys already lying there got pushed further out past the ramp. I gritted my teeth as Matt rolled up the street and once again turned around, pedaling towards the ramp. We were nervous watching the bike go over us, but Matt cleared it. He cleared seven kids. After a few more jumps, Matt decided he would tweak the ramp. Fortunately for us, we got called in for dinner before his next exhibition.

After dinner, we quickly cleaned up and raced into my room.

"Why did you volunteer for the jump?" I asked. Monique wasn't overly adventurous, nor did she like to get dirty, so I was surprised when she volunteered.

Monique shrugged her shoulders but didn't say much.

Looking at Monique, Tia piped up, "Somebody has a crush."

"I do not!" Monique's cheeks began flushing before she got the words out.

Tia and I began chanting, "Matt and Monique sitting in a tree, K.I.S.S.I.N.G., first comes love, then comes . . ."

Monique punched me in the arm before I could finish, "Shut up. I do not." She rolled her eyes at Tia and me.

"He is cute," Tia said. "Do you think he will be riding his bike tomorrow? Maybe we can help with his new ramp."

"Well, I don't see him that much, and I don't know him well," I responded with reservation. Changing the subject, I put on my *Saturday Night Fever* album so we could dance. Next, we played jacks before deciding to have a hula hoop contest.

Harry checked on us several times. I jumped as the door flew open. One time he asked, "What are you girls doing in there?" A second time he asked, "Are you thirsty?" A third time he knocked and asked, "Do you want some ice cream?"

"Does he always do that?" Monique asked.

"What?" I said, looking over at her.

"Just open the door like that? He has checked on us like five times. What does he think we are doing?"

I shrugged, thinking about it, "Actually, he doesn't usually do that."

"That's weird," she said, rolling her eyes.

Finally, Harry asked if we wanted to play Atari. The Atari was new, and we had just gotten the game *Pong*. Playing a video game at home was a new thing. Before, we could only play games like that at the arcade, and we rarely got to go there. The three of us each had two turns before heading to the room for good.

Before I closed my door, I called out, "Don't come in here. We are going to change into our pajamas."

"We won't." Mom's voice came down the hallway. "Goodnight," she called out as she and Harry went into the backyard to smoke.

The next day, Monique had to be home before ten o'clock to do her chores. After breakfast, the girls helped me finish my chores, and I was allowed to accompany them to Monique's house. She lived a few blocks past Tia. We walked comfortably together, stopping at Tia's on the way so she could check in with her mom and drop off some of her things. My mom had given me twenty dollars so we could go out for lunch. Next to Big Lots on Lake Murray, there was a diner that didn't have a name; it just had a big sign above the door that said Restaurant. We headed there after we helped Monique with her chores.

Monique's stepfather owned a barbershop, and there was a competitor's shop near Big Lots, so he asked her to walk by there and see if there were a lot of customers in that shop. After cruising by the barbershop, she called her stepdad from a payphone and gave him an update on the competition. Monique said he drove by that shop several times a day to see how busy they were. I found this to be hilarious.

Spying complete, we ate and went into Big Lots to look around before all of us had to head back to our own houses. I still had a few dollars to spend. I wanted some Lip Smackers and a ring, but I only had enough money for the Lip Smackers. As I internally argued with myself about what to choose, Tia and Monique came and pulled me urgently down the next aisle. Bart and Stuart from our class at school were walking outside the store.

Snatching the Lip Smackers from me, they yanked me down to the cash register, saying, "Hurry, we want to see where they are going." Tia hung her head out the door to see them. In our rush, I left the store with the ring still on my finger.

"They went this way. Come on." Tia pulled Monique along until the boys stopped and turned into a sporting goods store.

"Move over." I backed up, pushing Monique as the three of us squished together, hiding behind cars. Trying not to be seen, we followed Bart and Stuart around the strip mall. We were unsuccessful. When the boys realized we were following them, they stopped mid-sidewalk, turned around, and stared at us. The three of us ran into a thrift store, embarrassed, and blamed each other for getting spotted.

"This was your idea." I pointed at Tia.

"Yeah, it was your idea," Monique said, following my lead.

This led to an argument about whose idea it was to follow them in the first place. We were each sure that we would be humiliated at school on Monday and therefore tried to disassociate ourselves from the whole event quickly. The consensus was that it was Tia's fault since there were three of us, and Monique and I agreed she was the odd one out.

We walked home, following behind Tia by about a hundred feet because she refused to talk to us. She didn't speak to either of us for the rest of the weekend.

As I reached the bottom of my street, I realized I had the ring on my finger. Guilt immediately showered over me like raindrops. There were some things in life that you just did not do, and stealing was one of them. I could hear Mom's voice ringing in my head, "Don't you ever take something that doesn't belong to you. One of the worst things you can be is a thief. I hate stealing. I have no respect for people who do that."

Not wanting to walk back to Big Lots, I looked at the ring, telling myself, "They have boxes of them. They won't miss it, and nobody is ever going to know. When you found $20 on the ground at the movies and tried to return it, Harry told you to keep it. He said that if you turned it in, the people at the lost and found window would just take it, so you should just keep it." All the justifications didn't make me feel any better. I walked into the house that afternoon carrying drops of guilt with a side of shame.

I couldn't sleep thinking about the ring. The next day, I asked Mom to take me to Big Lots when she went to the grocery store.

"You just went there yesterday," she retorted.

"I know, but I need a folder, and Tia had to be home, so I didn't have time to get it." I did need a new folder because mine had gotten torn. I showed my worn-out folder to Mom, and she agreed to replace it. As we walked down the aisle towards the folders, I cut over one row to the box of rings and dropped the one I had worn home back into the basket.

REFLECTIONS

Childhood Friendship

In the article "The Importance of Childhood Friendships,"[5] the author credits childhood friendship with promoting emotional growth, good mental health, and a sense of security. Andrea's friendships with Tia and Monique carried her through some of the most difficult years of her childhood.

Fun Fact: Andrea and Tia are still friends.

---

[5]   Uzma Ahmad, "The Importance of Childhood Friendships," Building Lives of Orphans from Morocco, August 5, 2018, https://bloomcharity.org/the-importance-of-childhood-friendships/.

16

SECRET SANTA

"**G**et out of the way," Drew said, pulling into the driveway.

I looked at him incredulously as he parked his new truck and impeded the four-square game Charlene and I were playing. Drew was an annoying roommate—there is no subtle way to say it. He was self-absorbed and not a kid-friendly person. Why my parents chose to take him into our home, I could not tell you.

"Don't hit my truck with that ball," he demanded, looking our way as he opened the sliding glass door that led to his room.

"Why are you parking in the middle of our game if you don't want the ball to hit your truck?" I retorted snottily.

Drew paused before closing the sliding glass door long enough to look at me and repeat, "Don't let the ball hit my truck." Then he shut the slider a little too hard.

I was not the only one who didn't appreciate Drew. After moving into Grandpa and Grandma's house, we got a dog and named him Pippin after a mischievous Lord of The Rings character.

After dinner this particular evening, we were watching *Charlie's Angels* together in the living room. Pippin positioned himself directly in front of the TV, facing Drew, blocking his view.

Drew slowly refocused his eyes from the show onto Pippin. After about ten seconds, Drew jumped up, ran into his bedroom, and began cursing up a storm. "Damn you, Pippin," he yelled from his room.

Drew was doing laundry while we watched the show so he would have clean clothes for his trip home for Christmas. He had carefully laid out his favorite blue windbreaker on the bed along with some other clothes not wanting them to get wrinkled. Pippin climbed onto his bed, pooped on his jacket, then sat in front of the TV until Drew noticed him and realized what had happened.

Another time, a similar scenario played out. As Drew complained to my parents, I couldn't stifle my laughter as I watched my mom look him squarely in the face and say, "You know what the solution is, don't you? Shut your door."

My sister and I had been strongly coached in a family meeting that if we went into the laundry room adjacent to Drew's bedroom, we must shut the door so Pippin could not get into Drew's room. Pippin was stealthy and didn't miss an opportunity when someone left the door cracked open, and Drew, unfortunately, left it open more often than not.

After a lot of complaining and rewashing of his jacket, Drew managed to get his things packed for his trip and left to catch his 6AM flight before we awoke. I couldn't help but relish the thought of spending Christmas vacation without Drew. No more parking his truck in the driveway or yelling at us about the dog going into his room. Two weeks of Drew free living felt like a welcome respite.

We eagerly welcomed the arrival of Christmas morning. "Are you awake?" Charlene gently pushed on my arm.

Turning over in bed, I viewed her gigantic grin.

"Come look. You are not going to believe it."

I threw my legs over the side of the bed and jumped up as my feet hit the floor in one fluid motion. I took my time following Charlene as she raced down the hallway and through the living room where I watched her rip open the sliding glass door as she sprung onto the patio. A ping pong table was set up on the patio with a huge red bow wrapped around it and four new paddles sitting on top.

"This is awesome," I screeched. "Let's see if Mom and Harry are up so we can play."

"Five minutes," Harry called out as we eagerly banged on their bedroom door.

"Hurry, we want to play ping pong," my sister and I sang out to the closed door.

"What?" I heard my mom say to Harry. "What are they talking about?"

My parents came out to the backyard and stared at the ping pong table, looking bewildered.

"Do you know who brought this?" Mom looked at Harry.

"No," he said as he walked to the side of the house and looked around. "Did you girls hear anything? Or see anybody come back here?" he questioned.

"No." We both shook our heads.

Charlene's eyes lit up as she very reverently spoke, "It was Santa Claus."

Andy and Steve Jones came by later that afternoon to wish us a Merry Christmas. "Oh, a ping pong table. How cool," Steve said as he looked at us. "Did your parents get that for you?"

"No, Santa did," we responded in unison.

"Do you know who did this?" Harry asked, waving his arm towards the table with eyes accusingly set towards Andy and Steve.

They looked at each other with blank looks. "Nope, I don't know," Andy answered. "You got paddles? Let's play."

We spent the afternoon eating pie left over from our Christmas feast and playing ping pong. As we cleared the plates, it occurred to me I hadn't spoken to my dad that day. His absence still stung, but amid celebrating with friends, I didn't feel the need to ruminate on it.

During the conversation happening over ping pong games, Mom mentioned her annoyance with Carrie, our after-school sitter. "She isn't prepping for dinner, and during the last week of school before the break, the girls didn't even finish their homework before we got home. Sometimes they have not taken their baths either. Do you know anyone who would be available and willing to take the job?"

"I'll do it," Andy piped up.

"Really?" My mom looked at him, surprised.

"Sure. I hang out around here anyway. I might as well make myself useful. Do you want me to be your babysitter?" Andy asked, looking at Charlene and me.

"Yes," we both replied.

The Monday after Christmas break when Carrie showed up after school, there two envelopes: one for Carrie and one for Andy. Carrie and Andy both arrived at our house around the same time. I remember feeling so awkward when Carrie picked up her envelope and opened it up, then looked at me and said, "Oh, I guess I got fired."

Looking at Andy, she barked at him, "You took my job?"

"All I know is Harry and Theda said they needed someone to watch the girls after school, and I said I would do it. Go talk to them if you have an issue."

Turning his back to her, he looked at Charlene and me and said, "Come on, let's go play pickle." Andy held the door open, and Carrie bounced outside.

As we watched her walk down the street towards her house, Andy stared over at me in a questioning sort of way. "Your mom didn't talk to Carrie before?"

"I don't know." I looked at him and shrugged.

"Man, that's cold-blooded," he murmured under his breath before looking up at me, smiling, and taking my glove. "Your it."

REFLECTIONS

Good Neighbors

The Jones brothers brought the ping pong table over and snuck it into the backyard in the wee hours of the morning. Harry was not working a lot of hours, and money was tight. The ping pong table brought hours of joy to Andrea and Charlene's family as well as a little Christmas magic.

17

PERFECTLY BROKEN

Memorial Day weekend arrived, and Scott Hudson and several members of the Jones clan decided to head over to Lake Murray and BBQ along with us. As Scott and Harry sat around smoking cigarettes in the small site we congregated in, Mom placed lunch atop the picnic table.

Andy came flying up on his motorcycle. "Jump on. Let's go for a ride."

I looked at my mom and asked if I could go. "I would rather you ride with Harry, but you can go if you want to," she answered flatly. Mom was not a big fan of motorcycles. I jumped on the bike with Andy before she could change her mind.

"I'll take care of her, Theda," Andy said before we took off, and I wrapped my arms around his waist to keep from flying off the back.

We rode close to the edge of the Lake, and the mud sprayed up behind us. The sultry rays and the breeze blowing through my hair felt like freedom. Andy was an experienced rider, and as he accelerated, he yelled, "Hold on tight!" and began swinging the back tire from side to side as we slid gracefully across the lake's muddy edge.

"Are you ok, or do you want to go faster?" he hollered over the wind.

"Faster," I screamed back as loud as I could. I had never been on a motorcycle, and I found it exhilarating. It birthed within me a similar effect as swimming but with more adrenaline. When I swam, everything just floated away. My mind quit ruminating, anticipating, and plotting ten steps ahead. As I pushed against the water and felt the slow flow of it overtake my limbs, it felt like stepping into another dimension. I could spend hours in the water. My spirit and soul became one with the rhythm of my heartbeat, and then my breath joined in. Stroke by stroke, I welcomed the water washing over me like a healing balm. It silenced my mind and helped it remain detached outside of this sacred space with its worries and stimuli, firing pain-inflicting messages. Even the secrets I carried couldn't weigh me down in the water—and boy, I had secrets. The ride, like the water, was a nice respite from my thoughts.

At dinnertime, everybody got a plate and plopped down in foldout chairs in the area we had claimed. I took my food and sat comfortably in a chair facing the water. As I glanced sidelong at our party, joking and laughing with one another, I listened to Steve strumming on his guitar, and my thoughts wandered. Being back at the lake with the group, my thoughts jumped back into overdrive. I didn't look at people the same way anymore, especially men.

It amazed me that Harry could show up and behave the way he always had as if nothing had happened. I suppose I was doing that too. My breath went shallow as I mentally left the lake, reliving the day everything changed.

Mom had taken a few days off from Barber College, and Harry had recently graduated and was starting a new job soon, so our family took advantage of the time. Little did I know it was the last outing of my childhood that would be carefree for me. We decided to take a drive to Julian and hike Stonewall Peak in Cuyamaca, then get some pie before the snow melted—apple boysenberry with crumb crust was my favorite. We brought bag lunches, paper plates, plastic cups, and a large thermos full of water. There was snow on the side of the road, so we stopped at a turnout and had a snowball fight.

Continuing towards Julian, the elevation increased and the tree covering fell away. Though it was colder as we neared Julian the warmth of the direct sunlight was melting the snow. It was a beautiful seventy-degree day with light wind and small fluffy clouds sprinkled across the sky. It couldn't have been more perfect.

Stonewall Peak was fun to hike, even though the trail was a bit muddy. The trail is 3.8 miles and goes in circles, looping around the mountain. Right off the bat, I got competitive and made a bet that I would beat Harry to the top. He was always willing to banter with me, and we both raced off as fast as our feet would carry us. Harry wasn't an incredibly athletic guy, but he moved deceptively quickly.

I tried to go off the trail and cut straight up the mountain as soon as Harry was out of sight, but my mom corralled me back onto the public trail and lectured me about safety before I got anywhere. She reminded me of the previous summer when I sprained my ankle while camping and told me she didn't want the inconvenience of looking for me to keep her from her post-hike reward of pie and ice cream. For good measure, Mom threw in the thought of snakes hibernating under rocks off the beaten path. She said they were just waiting to sink their fangs into unwitting hikers who don't follow the rules. I had sprained the same ankle three times in one year, so it was a legitimate concern.

I took off up the loop and caught up with Harry at the top. We waited for Mom and Charlene, then got out our bag lunches and our thermos of water from the backpack Harry was carrying. The view from the top looked spectacular. As I sat on a rock inhaling the musky scent of earth and pine, watching my family eat chips and peanut butter sandwiches, I felt such a sense of peaceful wonder. I didn't want the day to end.

Harry and I collided at the bottom of the trail in our race to the finish. As predicted by Mom, I tumbled over Harry and twisted my ankle. She still had a wrap in her purse from my last mishap, and without a word, she pulled it out and wrapped my foot. Harry got the bonus of carrying me to the car since he failed to listen to my mom and stop behaving like a child.

I taunted him all the way there. "You aren't tired, are you? It's only one more mile to the car."

Mom and Charlene giggled as Harry threatened to leave me on the road.

Mom's Apple Pie was a favorite restaurant, and it didn't disappoint us. Harry and Mom had coffee with their pie, and Charlene and I got hot apple cider. Julian was bustling with people. A family generously moved over to share their outside bench with us when they saw my injured foot, and that I was having trouble standing as we waited for a table to become available.

"See, it came in handy," I jeered at my mom, pointing down at my foot.

She rolled her eyes and turned her head in the other direction towards Harry. Swinging her thumb back towards me, she said, "I suppose we won't be able to window shop with gimpy here."

"I suppose not," he responded.

Unable to browse through the town, after getting our fill of pie, we drove home feeling content.

At the lake when I recalled the fun we had that day, I felt a profound sense of sadness in my heart, knowing that for me, life with my family would never be like that again.

After we arrived home from Julian, I went into the backyard and lay on a lawn chair in the sunshine with the latest Nancy Drew book in tow. The afternoon was fading away, but the sun was still out, and I didn't want to miss it. Mom suggested a simple dinner of hot dogs and chips. After our afternoon of gluttony in Julian, nobody wanted a heavy meal.

When it got dark, Harry lit a backyard bonfire. Stars permeated the evening sky, and we sat outside, enjoying the ambiance. Mom had found an extra wide lounge chair at a yard sale, and it was really comfortable.

Harry plopped himself onto it with a box of Oreos in his hands.

"Hey, we wanted to sit there," Charlene and I hollered as we jumped on Harry's lap and pushed our way onto either side of him.

As I reminisce, I wonder if things would be different now if we had not jumped into the chair with him. My thoughts recalled the evening air cooling and the temperature dropping quickly after the sun had set. Mom brought out blankets and tossed one to Harry, who spread it over the three of us in the lazy lounger, and Mom took one to cover herself in the foldout chair she sat in. She also brought a lantern and a well-worn copy of the Hobbit.

As Mom read aloud, I was transported into the world of lush rolling hills with curious creatures called Hobbits who like routine and order and lived in underground homes. As a wizard arrived, disturbing the peace with the threat of an adventure, I was shocked out of my revelries of Hobbiton and carried into the present.

Every detail is still so clear in my mind now. I wore shorts and a t-shirt, and as I sat across from my mom, listening to her read, Harry put his fingers down my shorts into my underwear. The shock of it made me jump, and without removing his fingers, Harry held me down onto the chair by my waist with his other hand and looked at me, saying "Stop wiggling around."

Mom looked up and said, "Knock it off, Andrea, unless you want to go to bed before the story is over."

My mouth fell open in shock as I gazed into Harry's eyes.

He sat there behaving as if everything was normal as he quietly pulled my ear close to his mouth and said, "Shhhhhhhh."

Grimacing with confusion, I couldn't believe what was happening. My mom was right there. I stayed stock still as she read the closing paragraph of the chapter, not hearing a word she said. My ears rang, and my thoughts were clogged.

I don't know how much time went by before my mom's voice abruptly shook me into the present, and her face came into focus. "Andrea, did you hear me? It's time for bed."

The feeling of being on autopilot enveloped me as I got up from the chair and walked to my room with my sister. I silently pulled off my clothes and put on my pajamas before crawling into bed, feeling perfectly broken.

"Andrea, come kick the ball with us." As I slowly left the video on replay in my head and came back to the present, I stared up at Andy, holding his hand out to me. I reached for it and let him pull me up from my chair. Normally I loved any kind of sports. The usual spark that I felt was missing, but I stepped toward the game anyway, not wanting to be questioned.

As we were splitting into teams, Mom directed Charlene and me. "Andrea, you go with Harry and Steve. Charlene and I will go with Andy and Scott."

"I want to go with Andy." I knew Mom was trying to force me to bond with Harry. She had noticed me pulling back from him. I had spoken on the phone to my dad recently, and she attributed my attitude to that.

"I want to go with Harry." Charlene hopped over the imaginary line that separated the teams.

We finished the day at the lake trying to keep the other team from getting the ball into our goal and vice versa. As a result of overzealous competition, some of us ended up in the lake. This prompted my Mom to pack us up and head home.

REFLECTIONS

Grooming Step Five: Sexualize the Relationship

Harry successfully completed the first five steps of the Grooming process. Now, the question is can he complete step six?

18

ANDY EXTRAORDINAIRE

ndy was a great kid-sitter. He was easygoing and patient with us. I don't remember him ever telling us to watch TV or trying to make us entertain ourselves. He wasn't reactive, and a special bond quickly developed between him and our whole family. Over the last six months, we had gotten to know him well, and we trusted him.

Even though it was June, the pool was still cold. We did not use the heater, so we had to wait for the warm summer months to swim in warm water. I frequently begged Andy to let me swim in the pool even though the water was fifty degrees. Regardless of the temperature, I would jump in and swim laps. He would leave me for five or ten minutes and then come out and say, "Are you cold?"

"Nuh, nuh, nuh, no," I would stutter back at him.

"Your lips are turning blue; come on out of there," he would say.

"Five more minutes, please, just fi, fi, fi, five more minutes," I would implore.

Andy figured out early on I would always ask for five more minutes. Knowing that, he started telling me it was time to get out about ten minutes earlier than the actual time I needed to get out. This allotted sufficient time for my negotiations.

In contrast to Carrie, Andy made quite an impression on my parents. Most of the time our homework was done, we took baths, got in our pajamas, and dinner was cooking before my parents got home. Mom left easy meals to prepare, like Shake-n-Bake chicken or macaroni and cheese and hot dogs. Andy would have the main course cooking, and Mom would get home and make broccoli or some other vegetable to go with it. He ate dinner with us frequently, especially when they had liver and onion night at his house, usually on a Friday. Andy told his parents he had to babysit and stayed late at our house eating pork chops.

Dad arrived in town unexpectedly. He had arranged with my mom to pick up Charlene and me from our house on a Thursday afternoon. Mom didn't tell us Dad was coming. It was a surprise. We heard a *"Rap Rap Rap"* on the door, and as I eagerly ran to answer it, Andy came flying through the kitchen to cut me off, blocking me with his arms as I reached for the doorknob and firmly said, "Do not open that door."

"But I," I started to retort, but he cut me to the quick.

"Step back. I've got it." Andy slowly opened the door to see a six-foot-five-inch tall man standing on the stoop towering over him and a 1965 root beer-colored Corvette Stingray parked in the driveway. "Can I help you?" Andy said, staring up at the man.

"Hi, I am here to pick up the girls," the deep baritone voice resonated pleasantly.

Taking a huge step backward, Andy responded with, "The hell you are," and promptly slammed the door, then shut and locked it in one smooth motion.

Charlene and I stood there with our mouths hanging open before going into fits yelling in unison, "That's our dad!"

"I don't care if it's Jesus Christ," Andy barked back. "He isn't leaving with either one of you until your mom tells me so, and she did not."

Peeking out of the curtained window built into the front door, I watched with no small level of angst as my dad's tall frame slowly walked toward his car. He repeatedly took a couple of steps, paused, began to turn back towards the house, stopped, then finally slid into his car, and pulled out of the driveway.

I sauntered back into the living room to see Andy lock the sliding door that led into the backyard and then run into Drew's room, securing that sliding door too. He then began checking the windows.

"You don't have to do all of that. He's gone," I said accusingly and a little too loudly as I sulked and watched Andy run from window to window.

"I'm sorry, but over my dead body is anybody leaving this house with either one of you girls unless your mom says so," Andy stated, firmly standing his ground.

As I sat there feeling dejected, wondering if I would see my dad at all, the phone rang.

Andy stepped into the kitchen and picked up the landline mounted on the wall, and I could hear the raucous laughter from my spot on the couch in the other room.

On the other end of the receiver, Mom was laughing so hard she couldn't speak. It took a good five minutes for her to get the words out. "I forgot to tell you that David was coming to pick up the girls. They have suitcases packed, sitting by the wall next to the door in my bedroom. He should be back in five minutes. Let him take the girls." She was still laughing when she hung up the phone.

I heard Andy muttering, "Oh great. He's coming back."

I don't believe Mom expected that boldness to come from a fifteen-year-old; however, it delighted her to see my dad challenged.

My father was a ship pilot. His sheer size caused people to take notice of him, but it wasn't only that. Dad had a presence about him that commanded respect. His peers referred to him as Captain, and he was not accustomed to being told off by a teenage kid. He most definitely did not expect to have the door slammed in his face. None of us expected that, but if there was ever any doubt, we knew then we were exceptionally safe in Andy's care.

Our suitcases were promptly tossed on the porch along with our jackets, so there was no reason for Dad to enter the house. With Dad's return, Andy briefly explained himself from a strategic location behind the screen door, stating that Mom didn't tell him he was coming. Dad acquiesced with a dry grunt and a nod, turning swiftly on his heel with a daughters' palm in each of his hands.

As we relaxed into the weekend with Dad, I went through a mock conversation in my head a million times: I would confide, "Dad, I need to tell you something about Harry."

Dad would wrap me in a blanket of fatherly concern, and he would take control of everything. I envisioned sharing with him what happened and then seeing his wrath ensue. Surely, he would swoop us up and insist we live with him. I fantasized about the kind of house we would live in and dreamed of decorating my room—in the chamber of my mind, I had it all figured out.

Once again, I dug down deep and mustered up my courage. As we wound down from the day and were ready for bed, I spoke up. "Dad, where would we live if something happened to Mom?"

His gaze set forcibly upon me, and as my eyes ferreted up at him, the storm I saw brewing behind the surface in his piercing blue eyes shocked me. The concern and gentleness I expected were masked underneath that look. He spoke evenly, "Andrea, you know I am out of the country eight months out of the year. Is there something wrong with your mom that I am unaware of? Is she sick?"

"Well, no," I stammered.

"I will always take care of you. You know that. I need you to try harder to get along with your mother. She loves you very much. You can't run away from your problems; the sooner you learn, the better. Your mom and I are divorced, and that is the way it is. Do you understand?"

"Yes," I spoke quietly, burying the notion that Dad would help me.

"I don't want to have this conversation again," he warned. He delivered this sentence with such an air of finality that it left me breathless.

Fizzling back onto the bed feeling confused, it took me some time to realize that Dad thought I was going to ask to live with him again. I should have gone back to tell him that wasn't what I was going to say, but I hadn't the courage. The thoughts began pouring over me like falling bricks. With a wounded spirit, I retreated into the comforter and tried to make sense of what had just happened.

I could tell him we could live with Aunt Valerie or Grandma Lambrecht. No, I didn't want to live with them. And what about my mom? What would happen to her? She was so sad when Dad left. What would happen to her if she found out about Harry? What if Harry left, and then it was only us and Mom again? I didn't want to go back to that either.

What happened with Harry was bad, but things were better at home with Mom since Harry came. After much contemplation, the great revelation dawned on me that if there was a problem, Dad didn't want to know. If your dad doesn't want to know, then who does?

The next day we had breakfast and loaded up the car to return home. When Dad dropped us off at home, he told Mom, "Theda, you have a good babysitter." This was an uncommon compliment coming from Dad. As unconventional as Andy was, even Dad knew we were safe with him.

REFLECTIONS

Trust & Communication

Andrea tried to tell her Father what was happening to her, but he failed to listen. He thought he knew what she was going to say and missed the opportunity to be there for her. After realizing that her father was not going to help her, Andrea cataloged her doubts and fears about the future. She ultimately decided not to speak up about the molestation that was happening.

What Andrea did have was Andy. He was a trustworthy person in Andrea's life who was kind, fun, and protective. Andy wouldn't know the impact that he had on Andrea until many years later.

You never know what those around you are going through. Just being caring and kind can make all of the difference in the world. You may never know how you have helped those around you.

According to a website[6] aimed at stopping sexual abuse, one out of three girls and one out of five boys are sexually abused before they are eighteen years.

---

[6]   "Facts and Stats about Child Sexual Abuse," Lauren's Kids, January 17, 2022, https://laurenskids.org/awareness/about-faqs/facts-and-stats/.

19

TANGLED MACRAME

Once school was out, a boy named Bobby Horton started hanging around when I was outside, always asking to play tag. He even played with my Barbie Go Styling Head, but then threatened to beat me up if I told anybody about it. One of his older brothers, Chuck, was just as pleasant. As we played tag outside, Chuck went into his garage, cracked the slatted window that advantageously faced my house, and used the sill to steady his BB Gun before shooting at us.

I ran inside with Bobby chasing behind me, trying to escape the onslaught of flying BBs. With my parents not at home, I told Bobby he had to leave my house and fend for himself because I couldn't have anybody inside the house.

Bobby stayed inside briefly to call his other brother to get him. David pulled his car out of their driveway and parked in front of my house. He stepped out of the car and opened his trunk.

Making room, he placed some macrame plant holders inside while calling to Bobby, "Get in the car."

"Is Chuck still in the garage?" Bobby said while tentatively walking down my driveway towards David.

"No, I told Mom what he did. He is in the house. Come on; I need to go."

"Where are you going?" Bobby asked.

"I need to get over to Vons and sell these plant holders so I can buy some more rope. I have two more orders."

"You made those?" I asked in awe at his creations.

Seeing my enthusiasm, David said, "Yes, I can show you how if you want."

"Really? Yes, I want to learn how to do that," I responded excitedly.

"Oh geez, can I just go home? I don't want to sell your stupid macrame. Take her with you. You two can geek out together," Bobby snottily retorted.

"Do you want to come?" David asked me.

"I can't. I am not allowed to go anywhere when my parents aren't home," I answered him, unable to hide my disappointment.

"That's ok. I will come by tomorrow afternoon and show you how to make a plant hanger. Ask your parents if it's ok."

David was cheerful in opposition to Bobby's pouty disposition. He told Bobby to go home and talk to their mom before saying goodbye and speeding off toward Vons.

The next day could not come fast enough. After being quizzed by my mom and Harry about David, they decided it would be all right for him to come over and show me how to make the plant hangers. I loved arts and crafts and bubbled with excitement to learn something new.

David came over, and after meeting my parents, he laid out all the materials on the kitchen table. He had a type of rope called cotton cord, timber rings, and beads. He began by pushing the strands of rope through the ring and tying it off. Next, he created a square knot and a ½ square knot, then showed me how to add beads. After he made a plant hanger, he assisted me with creating one. After much direction and help with my technique, by the afternoon's end, I had a finished product.

"You caught on quick," David encouraged me. "Would you like to go into business with me?"

"Really?" I was delighted. "What do I need to do?"

"Well, I have the product to get us started. You will need to create one plant hanger every day, and on Saturday or Sunday, we will go to Vons and set up a table to sell them. With our earnings, we will buy more products so we can keep making the plant hangers. We won't make a lot at first, but after a few weeks, we will have enough material to start making a profit. If we put 25% back into materials, that will give us 75% profit. So, if you sell each of your plant hangers for $15 dollars you will make about $11.00 on each one, and you will put $4.00 back into the pot for materials. When you get better at making these, I will show you how to make the bigger size. You can sell those for $25."

After a discussion with mom and Harry, they gave me the green light to join David. They said I could make one plant hanger a day if I did not neglect my chores. I worked tirelessly at perfecting my knots and learning how to properly tie off the hanger at the top. I managed to create five macrame hangers with the material David left me.

After week one, we collected our goods and headed out to Vons. We sold all our plant hangers, and David said we could make a profit because he had more material on hand than he initially thought. David carried all the materials over to my house so he could help me throughout the week because I couldn't go to his house, nor did I want to, considering who his brother was.

Harry was skeptical about David's good nature and his willingness to help me get started and frequently said so. "What is he getting out of this?" Harry asked me. "Where are you keeping the money?"

"I don't know," I answered. "David is taking care of it."

"Oh, leave it alone, Harry," my mom chimed in. "He is just a kid."

While working with David one day, I told him that Harry had said that he was trying to get free labor out of me and rip me off.

"What?" David said, looking down at me. "I put up all the material, and I taught you how to make the hangers for free. Do you think I am trying to rip you off?" he asked, looking intently at me.

"No, I don't," I answered him.

"Look, I just saw how interested you were and thought you would have some fun with it, that's all."

I looked at my feet, confused and feeling bad that I had told him what Harry had said.

"How about if we keep the money for the materials at your house? He will feel better about it then," David suggested.

When Harry got home, I happily told him David said we would keep the money for the business at our house and showed him our bounty. After selling our second bunch of planter hangers, which David did without me because Harry said I had to stay home with my sister that day, David and I had each taken $4.00 in profit. That left $16.00 in the basket.

Making my own money from what I created was such an empowering experience. I worked diligently and looked forward to the weekend to sell our products. Harry showed a lot of agitation about my business and constantly tasked me with other things when he saw me making planter hangers. Mom, on the other hand, was incredibly supportive of it. That seemed to bother Harry even more.

At the end of the third week, David and I went to Vons and sold our goods. I didn't make as many that week as I had prior because Harry didn't allow me the time. Still, I had four to sell. Enthusiastically, I bounced into the house and retrieved the basket so we could divvy up our profit and put our percentage back in for business materials. When I opened the basket, the money was gone. Looking around at David, my face fell. "The basket is empty," I said while turning it so he could see it.

When Harry strolled in from the backyard, I looked at him and said our money is gone from the basket.

"Oh yeah, I had to borrow that," he said.

David looked up at him. "That was for our business materials."

"Yeah, I will get it back to you on payday. I needed gas and cigarettes, and I was short."

When I walked with David outside, he looked at me and said, "Harry had no right to take our money."

That ended our business arrangement.

REFLECTIONS

Grooming Step Six: Control and Conceal the Abuse

Harry was immediately agitated when Andrea began her business with David. With David around so often, there was less opportunity for abuse to happen. Harry also felt threatened by the mentorship David was developing with Andrea. He feared that she might tell David about the abuse; therefore, did everything he could to sabotage the business and was eventually successful.

20

A BIRTHDAY & A BICENTENNIAL

"Here, open this one." Charlene handed me a neatly wrapped wallet-sized present with a red bow and ribbon dangling off the sides. It was an autograph book.

Andy and Steve came over after we finished eating cake in honor of my ninth birthday. After collecting some signatures in my book, Steve serenaded me with a rendition of "Happy Birthday" on his guitar.

With the crew relaxing inside, I went out front to practice cartwheels on the grass. Andy followed behind. I looked across the street and saw his parents sitting on their driveway in lawn chairs with drinks in their hands. They had lit their BBQ, and I smelled hamburgers cooking.

"Do you think they would sign my autograph book?" I asked, looking back at Andy.

"Come on," he said, briskly heading for his house.

I ran inside to grab my autograph book then hurried to follow him to his driveway. He stopped near his dad and looked over at me.

I stood there, mouth clamped shut.

"Well?" he stated, nodding his head towards his dad, and then went into the house, leaving me standing there, book in hand.

Matt and Andy had shared stories about Mr. Jones being a no-nonsense kind of man. When I was left to fend for myself, I felt intimidated. I expected a gruff response to my request, and as I looked at Mr. Jones, he viewed me with an unreadable expression on his face.

"Um, it's my birthday, and I got this book, and I um, well, do you think you could sign it for me?" I sputtered as I held the book out for him to view.

"You want my autograph?" he asked.

I stared at him and nodded to keep from stuttering and embarrassing myself any further.

"Well, come on over here, little lady," Mr. Jones said, patting the chair beside him. "Do you have a pen?" he inquired.

"Uh, no, I don't." I stared down at the driveway.

"Carolyn, would you get this little lady a pen," he called out to his wife, who was standing in the garage with a pitcher in her hand, pouring a cup of iced tea into a glass.

Bob Jones got everybody that was home to sign my book, then attached the pen to one of the pages using the cap and told me to hold onto that for future autographs. Andy returned and told his parents he was watching my sister and me for two or three hours. His mom signed my book, *To a great little swimmer, Carolyn Jones*, and Mr. Jones just penned his signature. After thanking Mr. and Mrs. Jones, we headed back to my house.

When Scott Hudson came over, he signed my book and ate some cake while my parents got ready to go. As we cleaned up the cake and straightened up the kitchen, Scott looked over at me and said, "Man, you are so lucky. You have the coolest parents. My parents were never fun like this."

My body stiffened involuntarily, but I recovered quickly and scrunched up my face looking at him, "I guess?" I responded, drawing out the words.

Scott was sweet, but I didn't want to hear what he was expressing. "You don't think so?" He threw the words out there like he was imparting some great pearls of wisdom I should deeply consider.

Annoyed, I shrugged my shoulders. "Uh, I don't know. They're just my parents."

Harry and Mom said their goodbyes with exultations to Andy about bedtimes and no more desserts.

Charlene and I skipped baths and put on our PJs. It was 1976, and the Summer Olympics were happening in July. *Wide World of Sports* had Evil Knievel on, and they were interviewing Nadia Comaneci during the episode.

Normally, I wouldn't have been interested in watching sports, but I loved watching gymnastics and couldn't wait to see her compete. Harry had explained what the Olympics were, and I spent a lot of time doing flips, backbends, and cartwheels, imagining myself as an Olympic competitor.

"How does she move her body like that?" I was in awe.

"Lots of practice. You can do that if you want to. It just takes practice," Andy said nonchalantly.

"What do you think, Charlene? Do you want to go to the Olympics?" Andy looked over at Charlene.

"I like the ice skaters," she replied.

"That's pretty cool, too. I like the downhill sleds."

Andy let us stay up thirty minutes past bedtime so we could finish watching the show. We sat on the couch eating birthday cake, and right as the show ended, we heard the car pull up in the driveway.

"Hurry, get to bed," Andy said, hurrying to the kitchen with our plates of cake.

Charlene and I skirted down the hall as quickly as we could and dove into our beds, pretending to be asleep. I heard Andy leave, and Mom peeked in to look at us like she always did. I felt her breathing on my face, and then she started laughing. "I knew you were awake" she said, looking down at me.

Charlene popped up in her bed and smiled. "You too?" Mom said, faking a grimace.

"How did you know?" I asked.

"You never go to bed without the night light on. I figured you didn't have time to turn it on because you were too busy jumping into bed. Get to sleep, birthday girl, and you too." She tussled Charlene's hair and turned the night light on before exiting the room.

I laid in bed thinking of what Scott Hudson said about my parents. Everybody liked Harry. He was funny and clever, always smiling, there with a listening ear, and seemed to slide in right when I needed a timely word. Harry loved to talk about politics and world issues, mostly about how the government was manipulating us. He had a lot of our friends mesmerized by his adventurous stories of train hopping. It all sounded so free and untethered—that was all the rage in the seventies.

Our home was a hub for many. If they only knew what was happening, I wondered how they would feel about Harry then. I also wondered if anyone would believe me should I speak out.

The 4th of July was no small celebration in the USA that year—America was two hundred years old, and that was all we had heard about for weeks. I would have to live 108 years to experience the tricentennial. Firework events happened all over San Diego, while sparklers fizzed and cherry bombs exploded around the neighborhood all day. Even though they were illegal, they were everywhere.

Harry bought some sparklers from Danny, and we played with them with delight. Mom and Harry discussed where we would watch the fireworks. Lake Murray had an event happening, and even though the 4th of July was on a Sunday, we had Monday off from school. The final consensus was that we would watch from our rooftop.

Mom directed, "Go get your sleeping bags, and you can wrap up in those to keep warm."

"We can even zip them together," Harry added.

I jerked my head up sharply as I responded, "I want my own sleeping bag."

Before Charlene could say anything, I pulled her by the arm into our room and told her, "Say you want your own sleeping bag or yours to be zipped together with mine."

"But I don't want to zip with yours," she said, looking up at me.

"Just do it," I snapped at her. Ever since that fateful night, I had anticipated what Harry might do, and I didn't want to give him an opportunity to get near my sister.

When the time came, we climbed onto the roof with help from Mom and Harry. Charlene got in between Mom and Harry but was inside her own sleeping bag, and I had a spot next to my mom.

"Don't walk around up here," Mom said as I attempted to get up and walk toward the snacks. Mom had some Styrofoam cups and a thermos of hot cocoa. We also popped popcorn and put it in paper bags.

Our radio was tuned in to the am station that played music coordinated with the firework show at Lake Murray. I bopped my head along to "Rollercoaster" by the Ohio Players. ABBA's "Dancing Queen" and a few other favorite tunes trilled out of the radio in perfect time with the show. The music got very patriotic at the finale, with "God Bless

America" playing to a firework displaying George Washington crossing the Delaware.

REFLECTIONS

Protecting Siblings

Andrea felt the need to protect her sister. It isn't shown a lot in the story, but there were uncountable hours spent by Andrea trying to manipulate her time so that neither she nor her sister would be in a position to be abused by Harry.

21

CAT & MOUSE

After that first time Harry touched me inappropriately, a few non-eventful months went by. Things were so normal that I began to wonder if I had imagined the whole thing. Then came a Saturday when Mom had an appointment. Before she left, Harry stood in the living room so I could see him from my seat at the kitchen table, but he stayed invisible from the hallway and opened his robe, exposing his naked body to me.

Helplessly, I felt the scraps left of my childhood fizzle away; I had a new normal, and there was no going back. Learning how to plan my time strategically so I would not be home without my sister when my mom wasn't there became commonplace. I was a master listener. As soon as I found out Mom would be gone, I made plans for myself or asked if someone could come over. I learned how everyone's footsteps sounded—I could tell the difference between Harry's *clop-clop* and Mom's *clink-clink* and Charlene's *pitter-patter*. Then I learned the sound the car made as it pulled into or out of the driveway. Unfortunately, I didn't always get it right, and occasionally, I was left stranded at home, alone, with him. That day was one of those days.

This brings us back to where we started this story. Knowing Mom was leaving, I went to lie down. I hoped I could fake sleep until she returned from her errands. You may recall that Harry had immediately entered my room and tried to wake me. I had effectively convinced him that I was asleep and then strained my brain, attempting to find a way to get to the phone without his knowledge.

Listening for several minutes, I heard nothing in the house and decided it was safe to open my eyes. Cautiously, I had turned my head toward the wall so he would not see my eyes open if he was watching me through the cracked bedroom door, only to connect eyes with Harry.

This game of cat and mouse continued throughout our life on Budlong Lake. Each encounter of sexual abuse brought a new level of knowledge for me to use in my attempts to avoid Harry's advances. Before this time, I had been tripped up because I thought he was gone and he was looking through the crack in the door. This time I learned never to open my eyes even if I felt he couldn't see me.

I believe that Harry realized I was evolving in my efforts to avoid him, and in his sick, twisted mind, he viewed it as a game we were playing together. I came to this conclusion because he would talk to me as if I was a willing party to his perversion, asking me what I liked and did not like, the way you would speak to a lover. He spoke to me as if we were conspirators having a torrid love affair instead of predator and prey.

Harry showed me things I didn't want to see. It made me feel dirty and ashamed. He would undress and ask me if I wanted to touch him. When I was unresponsive, he would take my hands and place them on himself as he explained male anatomy to me. He asked if I understood what sex was and proceeded to explain how pregnancy happens, listing the parts of female anatomy while he touched mine.

I went to great lengths to keep the abuse a secret. I had watched a show on *60 Minutes* about girls who were being molested and how they suddenly became uninterested or withdrawn. Some had uncharacteristic outbursts or became brooding and moody, radically changing their appearance. I also became alerted that certain behaviors would signal to my teachers something was wrong. Knowing that I couldn't appear too tired or let my grades fall, I made intentional efforts to keep everything the same. No noticeable changes that would attract attention could be indulged.

Though I desperately wanted to tell someone what was happening, I was afraid of what it would do to my family. What would happen to Mom? Would she be alone again? Once I knew living with Dad wasn't an option, I felt I didn't have anyone to tell. I had considered telling Andy about what was happening, but before I found the courage to do it, Harry wasn't working. Andy wasn't coming over to watch us as often, and though the connection and trust were still there, there was less opportunity.

Fear of the unknown was also a factor that kept me quiet. In that way, Harry spoke to me like a lover; he told me that if anybody found out about "us," they would not understand. He suggested they would take Charlene and me away from our home and our friends. We might even go to foster care where Charlene and I could get separated. Who "they" were, I didn't know.

Ironically, I even worried about what would happen to Harry if I told. So, for all of these reasons, I didn't.

Despite my best efforts, the stress of it all had to come out somewhere. I began having out-of-body experiences when I went to sleep and would view myself as if I were outside my body. Levitating, I could see everything from an aerial view. I observed my mom in the kitchen, Harry watching TV, and

Charlene skipping rope in the backyard—and I could see myself sleeping on my bed.

During these encounters, I would speak to a man who reminded me of my grandfather. He was very soft-spoken and kind. I poured my soul out to him, and he listened intensely. When I was awake, I spent so much time fitting in and making no waves, but when I was there, I was seen. He seemed to know what was happening without my explanation, but he listened if I wanted to talk. I found his presence to be of great comfort.

The man didn't pretend like things weren't difficult, nor did he try to fix anything. He had a way of acknowledging the struggles and convincing me I was going to be okay. We had long conversations about my interests and my dreams, and we laughed the careless laughs of people with no burdens. He exhorted me not to let my dreams die and told me I had an incredibly special purpose in the world.

Many descriptions of this type of phenomenon have been told, and people have tried both to define and discount it. Some say my mind created it all to deal with the stress of what was happening to me. Others say it was an angel. I just know that I am grateful for an older man with a listening ear who appeared to a little girl who desperately needed a male figure she could trust. I was isolated and hiding in plain sight, and whatever it was that happened, it gave that troubled girl a little slice of peace.

Eventually, Grandma and Grandpa came back to their home, and we left Budlong Lake. The Jones family left first, moving to Mira Mesa. Shortly after they left, we moved to a small cottage on Park Blvd. We kept in touch with most of our friends from there. Our lives would continue to intertwine with the Jones family but that is another story.

Shortly after we moved, Harry accepted a job opportunity overseas working for Grandpa. That left Mom, Charlene, and

I living alone for a year. By the time Harry returned, I was too old for him to continue molesting. I kept my silence, but it had a price, and eventually, everybody would pay it.

REFLECTIONS

Grooming Step Six: Control and Conceal the Abuse

Throughout Book 1: *I Am Not Your Prey*, Harry was able to control and conceal the abuse.

Divine Intervention

"For he will command his angels concerning you to guard you in all of your ways." (Psalms 91:11-12, NIV)

Andrea did not share what was happening to her with another living soul, but she was not left alone. The out-of-body experience gave her the strength she needed to survive what was happening to her.

SHATTERING SHAME SERIES

Book 2: The Prey Takes Flight (Preview)

I stood above him with the cast iron pan raised high above my head, holding the weight of it with both hands. I could bring it down on his head, but was I strong enough? If the blow didn't knock him unconscious, he would get up and kill me. What if I killed him? Would a jury send me to prison? He had consumed a fifth of Jack Daniels, and as I stared at him passed out on the couch, all I could think was, "This is my chance." I had not left the house in three weeks, and neither had Billy. I was beginning to think that I might die there. It might be the only opportunity I got.

Setting the pan down, I grabbed the few dollars I had, heart beating wildly, and slid into the bathroom. Slowly, I opened the sliding window above the bathtub one inch at a time so he wouldn't hear it. Stepping onto the built-in soap dish, I stood up and squeezed my one hundred-and eight-pound frame through the tiny window. I landed silently like a cat on the grass. Before I could think another thought, I ran.

There was a hole in the middle of the backyard fence board, creating a knot I could fit my toes into. Using that hole, I awkwardly thrust my leg up to the top of the fence. I had more strength in my legs than I did in my arms, so I allowed the fence to scrape my leg as it went over in order to shift my weight enough for me to use my arms to propel the rest of me after it. I fell seven feet and landed on my back.

Taking a moment to catch my breath, I ran gasping through the neighbor's side yard and opened the gate, revealing the sidewalk. Running up the sidewalk and across the street, I trespassed through another neighbor's side yard so I could hop their backyard fence to get to the street bordering Black Mountain Road. There were lots of windows on that house, though, and the occupants stared at me wide-eyed. But I knew if I could make it to Longs Drug Store, I could use the phone and wait for help in a public place. Calling the police wasn't an option—Billy had made it clear what would happen if I did.

As I raced through their yard, I dragged a small plastic table next to their fence and stepped on it before heaving myself up and hopping over. I couldn't stop. There wasn't time to explain and apologize. Asking for their help would put them in danger if Billy was chasing me.

Billy wasn't rational when he was angry; after the alcohol he consumed, he wouldn't be easy to reason with. There was a shift in Billy over the last month. I didn't know what was going on, but things were out of control.

My parents had moved from San Diego to a very rural place called Warner Springs in my sophomore year of high school. After three months of one and a half hour bus rides each way to and from school I was done with it. I put my books into my school locker after school one day, walked out to the road, and caught a ride to San Diego with some lumberjacks. My mom signed emancipation papers shortly after that, and I moved in with Billy. The empowerment I felt leaving the home where my stepfather resided was indescribable.

The first few months living with Billy were very freeing, but I traded some of my childhood for adult responsibilities, and I had already lost so much. In many ways, I had jumped out of the frying pan into the fire—I was rethinking that decision with regret.

We had roommates—Ryan and Debra—but they weren't home. Billy's behavior, as of late, had created a lot of tension in the house, so they were spending the weekend away.

It was an adjustment being the only one still in high school. Everybody else was adulting already, and I felt pressure to follow suit.

Trying to ease my tension, I took a deep breath before heading up the street. All I had to do to get to Longs was go around a corner, walk about a quarter of a block, and then cross Black Mountain Road. I was almost there. My plan was to call my best friend Jo and see if she and Rolf could pick me up and take me to my mom's house in Warner Springs. Billy would go straight to my grandparent's house, so I couldn't go there.

I was winded by the time I got to the light. As I waited for the traffic to clear enough to run across the street, I heard the familiar rumble of the Dodge Challenger's deep groaning motor. With dread in my heart, I turned my head to see the passenger door open and Billy in the driver's seat, pointing for me to get in.

STUDY GUIDE

Use the questions to work through your feelings, and don't rush. Healing comes a little bit at a time, and joy comes in the morning.

STUDY GUIDE QUESTIONS

Chapter 1

1. Have you ever disliked someone because they have similar characteristics or personality traits as a person who hurt you?
2. Due to the abuse she endured; Andrea grew up very quickly. She was constantly analyzing and anticipating the future.
   A. Did you grow up with any circumstances that caused you to take on more responsibility than was age appropriate?
   B. What effect(s) did that have on you?

Chapter 2

1. Have you experienced the loss of a parent through a divorce? Or death?
   A. How did that affect you? Did you feel abandoned? Angry? Afraid?
   B. If so, who were those feelings directed at?
   C. How did those feelings manifest themselves?
2. Did the parent you lived with eventually marry or date another person?
   A. Did you accept that, or did you resent it?
   B. How did you express your feelings about that?

Chapter 3

1. Has a parent or guardian behaved in a way that was questionable when you reflect back on it?
   A. Was the action acceptable when it was done but is now commonly rejected?
   B. Are you currently judging that person for their past actions?
2. Andrea behaved poorly, letting her hurt drive her to retaliate in anger.
   A. When you were a child, did you ever behave in a way you were ashamed of?
   B. Did you understand why you behaved that way?

Chapter 4

1. Where did you feel safe when you were a kid?
   A. It could be an actual place, or perhaps you felt safe with a particular person.
   B. Where do you feel safe now? With whom? Or where? Or doing what?
   C. When I _____________ I feel safe.

Chapter 5

Harry added value to Andrea's life by addressing a tense situation between her mother and grandmother. He changed the dynamics between them, and it made a significant impact.

1. Nobody starts a relationship by abusing another person. How did a person that abused you initially add value to your life?

Chapter 6

1. Andrea's family went on a vacation that created cherished memories for her.
   A. What life events created good memories for you?
   B. How can you use those memories to help foster good feelings?

Chapter 7

1. Did your family ever relocate when you were a kid?
   A. If so, what was good about it? If not, what was good about growing up in the same place?
   B. What was challenging about it?
   C. What did it teach you?
   D. How can you use that to your benefit?

Chapter 8

1. Andrea had always believed she had the choice of living with her father. The reality was that she did not have that option, and when she was faced with the truth, she felt deflated.

A. Was there a time in your life when you thought you had options but truthfully, you didn't?
B. How did you manage that? Did you get depressed? Did you sulk? Did you lash out?
C. How do you handle disappointment today?

Chapter 9

1. Andrea desired a connection with her father, but she didn't know how to get it.
    A. Do you have a close relationship with your father? (This could be a stepfather, guardian, or an important male figure in your life.)
    B. What do you like about the relationship?
    C. What can you do to improve it?

Chapter 10

1. Did you ever pull a prank, or play truth or dare when you were a kid?
    A. What kid games got you into trouble?

Chapter 11

1. Andrea felt imposed by the burden to care for her younger sister.
    A. Do you have siblings or cousins that impacted your life growing up?
    B. If yes, how was that dynamic between you growing up?
    C. How do you think it shaped the person you are today?

Chapter 12

1. Where did you live when you were growing up? Did you
    stay in one place or move around?
    A. What places impacted you the most?
    B. Why?

Chapter 13

1. Andrea's neighborhood had a close-community feeling
    that is rare today.
    A. Is there a place in your life that gives you that sense
        of belonging? A church, a family member's home, a
        team, or a club?
    B. If so, can you identify what brings that sense of
        connection?

Chapter 14

1. Andrea's mother had the gift of hospitality. She made
    their home welcoming and fostered an environment that
    people were drawn to.
    A. Was your home welcoming? If yes, what gifts were
        imparted or displayed that you can imitate to create
        a welcoming environment?
    B. If not, who do you know that has qualities you admire?
        What can you learn from them?

Chapter 15

1. Did you ever do something you felt guilty about, like
    Andrea did with the ring?
    A. What was your response?
    B. Why?

Chapter 16

1. Andrea's family got a great surprise on Christmas day.
    A. Has there been a time when you received an unexpected surprise?
    B. How did it make you feel?
    C. Is there someone in your life that could use a secret surprise?

Chapter 17

1. In this chapter, it is revealed that Andrea is carrying secrets. Swimming was her safe place/activity.
    A. What is yours?
2. Andy made Andrea feel protected.
    A. Who makes you feel protected?
    B. Who made you feel protected when you were a kid?
3. Andrea tried to confide in her dad, and it blew up in her face.
    A. Have you ever tried to tell somebody something difficult and had it work out poorly?

Chapter 18

1. Harry's actions ended Andrea's creative business opportunity and impacted her friendship with David.
    A. Have you ever lost something because of somebody else's actions?
    B. How did it make you feel?
    C. Have you forgiven that person?

Chapter 19

1. Harry was sexually abusing Andrea, but the neighbors and friends thought he was a great guy. When we think of child molesters, we think of shady, unclean people. We don't think of our next-door neighbors. The truth is most people are molested by someone they know, not a stranger.
    A. Why do you think nobody suspected anything was happening?

Chapter 20

1. Andrea had grown to love Harry as a father figure. He spent a long time gaining her trust, and then he betrayed that trust in one of the worst ways.
    A. Has anyone betrayed your trust?
    B. Is it difficult for you to trust people now?

Chapter 21

1. Andrea had out-of-body experiences that helped her deal with the stress of being abused.
    A. What helped you?

Check out the BONUS CONTENT
http://authorandreasjones.com

FINAL NOTE

I hope this book has shined a light on how grooming happens and brought some clarity. Admittedly, there are a lot of feelings that go along with that. Maybe some memories or realizations have surfaced about why you are the way you are. None of that is to be feared.

Feel free to peruse my website or take my course. I would love to hear from you and personally walk you through my process of finding freedom after sexual abuse. Find more information at authorandreasjones.com.

Now that we are at the end of the book, there is one question that you must ask yourself:

Why are you ashamed of what somebody else did to you?

Photo taken by Tamara Trujillo

www.ingramcontent.com/pod-product-compliance
Lightning Source LLC
Chambersburg PA
CBHW031318160726
47993CB00001B/459